Renewing Your Mind
in a Secular World

Renewing Your Mind in a Secular World

Edited by John D. Woodbridge

MOODY PRESS

CHICAGO

All Scripture quotations, except those noted otherwise, are from the
New American Standard Bible, © 1960, 1962, 1963, 1968, 1971, 1972,
1973, 1975, and 1977, by the Lockman Foundation and are used by
permission.

Scripture quotations marked (NIV) are from the *Holy Bible, New International Version.* Copyright © 1973, 1978, International Bible Society.
Used by permission of Zondervan Bible Publishers.

Scripture quotations identified with the letters (WK) are from transla-
tions prepared by Walter C. Kaiser, Jr.

The use of selected references from various versions of the Bible in this
publication does not necessarily imply publisher endorsement of the
versions in their entirety.

Library of Congress Cataloging in Publication Data
Main entry under title:

Renewing your mind in a secular world.

   Includes bibliographical references and index.
   1. Christian life — 1960-   — Addresses, essays,
lectures. 2. Spiritual life — Addresses, essays,
lectures. 3. Meditation — Addresses, essays, lectures.
4. United States — Moral conditions — Addresses, essays,
lectures. I. Woodbridge, John D., 1941-
BV4501.2.R46   1985   248.4   85-10677
ISBN 0-8024-0384-0 (pbk.)

      1 2 3 4 5 6 7 Printing/BC/Year 90 89 88 87 86 85

Printed in the United States of America

Contents

71049

Introduction

by John D. Woodbridge

It is a bewildering paradox that one-third of all American adults claim to be born again and yet fail to impact our society which becomes sicker and more corrupt by the day. Religion is up but morality is down.

Charles Colson

America in 1984 appears to be confronted with a great paradox: Religion is growing in importance among Americans but morality is losing ground.

George Gallup, Jr.

Charles Colson presents us with a troubling paradox: "Religion is up but morality is down." Why is it that we as evangelical Christians (one-third of the adult population) have not influenced our society's morality as much as our numbers suggest that we might?

It is not because many of our brothers and sisters in Christ have shied away from the challenge. A growing number of Christians are, in

John D. Woodbridge (B.A., Wheaton College; M.A., Michigan State University; Ph.D., Université de Toulouse, Toulouse, France; M.Div., Trinity Evangelical Divinity School) is professor of church history at Trinity Evangelical Divinity School, Deerfield, Illinois. He is co-editor of *The Evangelicals* and *Scripture and Truth* and has written *Biblical Authority: A Critique of the Rogers and McKim Proposal* and coauthored *The Gospel in America.*

fact, tackling the social and moral ills of society. Some have sought public office in the hardfisted political arena. They hope to bring about structural changes in our society through legislation. Others have organized special interest groups whose clout is considerable. Still others have ministered to the physical and spiritual needs of the downtrodden.

Christians have become more involved in various communication fields. They have launched many new radio and television stations within recent years. Evangelical printing houses have produced excellent helps for studying the Bible. The harvest of new Bible versions, commentaries, and dictionaries is so plenteous that most of us can only sample portions of it. We are also witnessing the growth of mega-churches that bring the faithful together by the thousands. The vitality of the evangelical movement in the United States is quite remarkable.

But despite the much-heralded "Evangelical Renaissance," Charles Colson's paradox does not vanish: morality *is* down. Since the early seventies, the tolerance of Americans for acts and attitudes the Bible designates as sin has increased. Not surprisingly, the word *sin* has almost disappeared in the public discourse of the nation's politicians, educators, and psychologists. Even a segment of the clergy refrains from using the word.

Many reasons could be suggested to explain the paradox, but two appear especially compelling. One is that a widespread spirit of resistance toward the ethical teachings of the Christian faith has emerged within our culture since the 1950s. Both subtle and direct attacks against the authority of the Bible have been mounted. In this day of radical pluralism a number of notable scholars cannot entertain the idea that any book could be the very Word of God or that any set of ethics has universal validity. Others are perplexed by the problem of determining what truth means as applied to a theological statement. In the name of separation of church and state and First Amendment rights, ACLU lawyers have attacked efforts to maintain as guiding principles for public morality ethical teachings that are specifically Christian. Professors at some of the nation's finest law schools make scant allusion to Judao-Christian standards as a basis for the development of law. Moreover, millions of Americans do not want to encumber themselves with the notion that the ethics of the Scriptures should direct their life-styles. They sense that adherence to biblical ethics would hinder an unrestricted pursuit of self-fulfillment. Many of the programs on the television networks and on cable TV feed a spirit of resistance to Christian values. The programs often depict sex outside of marriage as normative and a materialistic life-style as desirable. Commercials stoke the fires of narcissism by pandering to the egos of the viewers. Many youth are giving their minds over to the sights and sounds of rock videos. Some of these videos revel in the occult, sexual perversity, and violence. In sum, "morality is down" because large numbers of Americans reject the notion that biblical ethics should mold their life-styles.

The second reason the influence of evangelical Christians upon the morality of American society is not as great as might be hoped concerns Christians more directly. Though evangelical Christians affirm that the Bible is an infallible rule for faith and practice, many of them compartmentalize their faith in such a manner that biblical teachings do not much affect the way they live on a daily basis. They profess sound evangelical doctrine but betray those confessions by their deeds. They do not consciously seek each day to live under the direction of biblical ethics.

As believers, we are not sheltered from the enticing messages of our society, nor are we immune from the intoxication of unrelenting activity. We may yield to those pressures far more than we ourselves sometimes recognize. It would be easy for a spirit of worldliness to have entered our very being.

Christ taught that Christians are to serve as salt and light in the world (Matt. 5:13-16). But salt can lose its savor, and a light can be dimmed. It is quite possible that we are experiencing a loss of spiritual power because we are not yielding ourselves to the Holy Spirit on a daily basis. Little wonder we have lost some of our saltiness and light. We cannot change the world because we are too much like it. The challenge of keeping a godly mind in modern America has overwhelmed us.

Our minds play an exceedingly large role in our Christian lives. It is in our minds that some of our fiercest spiritual warfare takes place. Even the stalwart reformer Martin Luther experienced victories and defeats in his thought life. We are not the first persons to wrestle with spiritual conflicts.

But the challenge of bringing every thought into the captivity of Christ is an especially difficult one today. Our minds are bombarded by conflicting messages coming to us through diverse media: television, radio, records, films, print, the plastic arts. A collage of impressions and ideas streams through our minds each day, leaving traces in our memories. Sometimes the messages we receive complement and reinforce our Christian convictions. On other occasions, the messages attack our moral standards and sap our spiritual vitality. Sometimes we notice their subtle but devastating effect upon our minds only after months and years have passed.

Today, the need for Christians to renew their minds through prayer, confession, meditation upon God's Word, and participation in the local church is paramount. The apostle Paul put the matter as a command: "And do not be conformed to this world, but be transformed by the renewing of your mind" (Rom. 12:2).

What specifically do Christians need to know about renewing their minds? This book attempts to answer that question. We have selected topics that are related to the general theme of renewing the mind. Certainly, there are other worthwhile subjects we could have chosen. We do not see this book as the last word on Christian spirituality. We see it as a means of encouraging Christians to "abide in Christ" and thereby retain their saltiness and light. We hope this book will help Christians to gain a greater appreciation of their heavenly Father's majesty and power and to sense more fully His tender love and compassion for His children.

This book is divided into three sections. The first describes in more detail the challenge Christians face in renewing their minds in today's society. John Woodbridge puts in bold relief the onslaught against the Christian's mind that has taken place since the 1950s. His historical sketch reveals dramatic changes in several values of our culture since that decade. Paul Meier, a medical doctor, emphasizes the importance of Scripture meditation for retaining mental and spiritual health. He argues that meditation on Scripture can help deflect a natural bent towards selfish and destructive thinking. The second section focuses on the Bible's teachings about renewing the mind. Walter Kaiser clarifies what biblical meditation is as distinguished from other types of meditation. Grant Osborne explains what renewing the mind involves from a biblical point of view. The third section describes in more detail the resources available to Christians as they meet the challenge of renewing their minds in daily living. David Larsen underscores the significance of the local church fellowship as an indispensable resource for the believer. Christians are not spiritual Lone Rangers fighting solitary battles with the Evil One, but members of the caring Body of Christ, the church. Grant Osborne highlights the importance of Bible study for developing a Christian mindset. He explains how a Christian can establish a meaningful devotional life. John Woodbridge sets forth Pastor Martin Luther's perspectives on knowing God. Luther generally maintained a confident trust in his heavenly Father even during times of depression and defeat. Luther's counsel concerning the Christian life is genuinely inspiring and highly practical. Doug Moo explains what bearing a renewed mind has upon the believer's day-to-day ethical decisions. He asserts that right living proceeds from a renewed mind.

A recurring theme runs through these essays: It is not we who renew our minds but the Holy Spirit who renews them for us. Only with the Holy Spirit's strength can Christians renew their minds in modern America and adopt a life-style that is pleasing to their gracious heavenly Father.

The gentle admonition of the apostle Paul to the Christians at Philippi sums up beautifully the life-style of those who constantly renew their minds through communion with their Lord:

> Be anxious for nothing, but in everything by prayer and supplication with thanksgiving let your requests be made known to God. And the peace of God, which surpasses all comprehension, shall guard your hearts and your minds in Christ Jesus. Finally, brethren, whatever is true, whatever is honorable, whatever is right, whatever is pure, whatever is lovely, whatever is of good repute, if there is any excellence and if anything worthy of praise, let your mind dwell on these things.

> (Phil: 4:6–8)

This God-ordained life-style is available to each one of us who knows Jesus Christ as Lord and Savior and who lives in the power of the Holy Spirit. By making it our own, we shall be able to cope better with life's tensions, trials, and temptations. We shall be able to serve other persons and the church with more serenity and spiritual power. And finally, we shall please the Lord God, to whom is due all glory and honor in this anxious and needy world and forever.

J.D.W.

Part 1
The Challenge of Renewing Our Minds in Modern America

1 The Contemporary Assault upon the Christian's Mind

John D. Woodbridge

America remains a land of great opportunity. Yet living a happy life today in the United States is a more elusive enterprise than it was even a generation ago. People are worried and with good reason. The nuclear family traverses rough seas, and the divorce rate repeatedly batters it.[1] Children skip their childhood, and teenagers seek to escape their troubles through suicide. Eighteen of our nation's teenagers commit suicide each day, and fifty-seven attempt it every hour. Despair has blighted their lives. Many young among our minorities believe that finding a job is a lost cause.

They have simply given up looking.

The drug culture is no longer confined to the back alleys and dilapidated tenements of America's big cities. Now it wreaks havoc in the entertainment industry and in professional sports. White parents have learned what black parents confronted long before them: their children can be exposed to a drug culture in the local schools. But youngsters cannot be tended every moment of the day. They must gain independence. The dilemma that parents face is a genuine one.

Then again, the parents of younger children fear that a twisted indi-

1. See Dean Merrill, "The Uncoupling of America: Why?" *Logos* 10 (September 1980): 20–23.

Portions of this essay were published originally in "Biblical Authority in a 'Me Decade,'" *Voices* (Winter 1984). Used by permission of the editor of *Voices*, a publication of Trinity Evangelical Divinity School, Deerfield, Illinois.

vidual might abduct a son or daughter straying away at a shopping mall. Between one and two hundred thousand youngsters disappear each year. Many older Americans find they can barely live on Social Security. Old age has not brought them honor and relaxation but rather heartache and loneliness. Those are some of the unpleasant realities of American life in the 1980s. They are not likely to go away in the future.

To cap things off, Americans today are sensitized to the idea that they may well face a nuclear day and its day after. Is any act of generosity or courage worth anything when recognized authorities lament that nuclear warfare is close to inevitable? Fear of a nuclear holocaust can push a person to seek the pleasures of the world today because there will be no tomorrow. It can shatter a person's capacity to dream dreams for a better day. It can lead a person to become depressed. Or it can provoke a person to make nuclear disarmament the overriding passion of his being. When fear of the outside world penetrates who we are, it drives out our capacity to enjoy even little pleasures: a crimson sunset, a baby's first smile. The living of a happy life seems a more elusive enterprise than it was even a generation ago.

Christians are not immune from considering themselves trapped by the concerns that trouble other citizens. The stresses and tensions that provoke anxiety for their neighbors are the same stresses and tensions they experience. Christian parents are concerned for the well-being of their children. They, too, worry about the crazed individuals who frequent shopping malls looking for unattended children. What Christian parents might not understand, however, is that their children face temptations not even imagined by teenagers in an earlier day. The tolerance, even outright approval, in America of sexual promiscuity makes it difficult for a young person to maintain high standards of morality. Moreover, the logistics of committing sin are more easily mastered today. Pornography is beamed into the living room, whereas in earlier days one had to search for it in sleazy theaters on the side streets of the nation's large cities. The average fourteen-year-old today has watched 11,000 murders on television and, as a result, experts complain, has become desensitized to violence.

The old securities that gave us confidence about the present and courage for the future seem to be vanishing. We are increasingly sojourners in a society that acknowledges rights but not the standards of right and wrong one used to assume all Judeo-Christian peoples espoused. An individual's rights are all that counts. The good is whatever he wants and can get; the bad is that which he lacks but wants. If someone believes that something is good for him, then it is good. Things and other human beings are disposable throwaways.

One's neighbor is made for one's self and is designed to serve one's needs. The idea burns like a flame in the heart of American culture. It eats up whatever or whoever gets in its way. Social commentators are at a loss to put the fire out.

As Christians, we are called to love the Lord our God with all our hearts, souls, and minds, and our neighbor as ourselves, in an age that is resolutely narcissistic. Little wonder that renewing the mind in modern America is no easy task.

THE NOT TOO DISTANT PAST

It would be silly to imagine that life in America was ideal in bygone days. Too many of us remember the frustrations we experienced in earlier years. If we are black, we certainly do not want to return to the days when the color of our skin created even more problems for us than it does today. If we suffered through the Depression we do not have much patience with those who speak of the thirties as the "good old days." If we have read about the twenties, we know that many corners of American life were penetrated by values alien to the Christian gospel. And yet—and yet. In decades not too far removed from us, the social fabric of the nation was held together more securely by Judeo-Christian values than it is today. There are a number of examples of the sense of propriety supported in earlier years. In a poll taken in 1924 in Muncie, Indiana, for example, respondents were asked if Christianity was the only true religion and if they thought everyone should be converted to it. Ninety-four percent of the citizens of Muncie agreed with those affirmations.[2] In 1931 the Supreme Court declared: "We are a Christian people according to one another the equal right of religious freedom, and acknowledging with reverence the duty of obedience to the will of God" (United States v. Macintosh).[3] It is doubtful whether the citizens of Muncie, Indiana, would still make the same assertions or that the Supreme Court would still speak of Americans as "a Christian people."

In 1934 the Motion Picture Producers and Distributors of America (M.P.P.D.A.) put a production code into strict effect in Hollywood. Films violating its principles faced a difficult commercial future. A listing of a few of those principles is instructive:

2. Daniel Yankelovich, *New Rules: Searching for Self-Fulfillment in a World Turned Upside Down* (New York: Random, 1981), p. 88.
3. Cited in *Eerdman's Handbook to Christianity in America,* eds. Mark Noll, Nathan O. Hatch, George M. Marsden, David Wells, and John D. Woodbridge (Grand Rapids: Eerdmans, 1983), p. 456. In preparing this essay, the present author relied upon some of his research for the fourth section of the *Handbook*.

The sanctity of the institution of marriage and the home shall be upheld. Pictures shall not infer that low forms of sex relationships are the accepted or common thing.

Excessive and lustful kissing, lustful embracing, suggestive postures and gestures, are not to be shown.

Pointed profanity (this includes the words God, Lord, Jesus, Christ— unless used reverently—Hell, S.O.B., damn, Gawd), or other profane or vulgar expressions, however used, is forbidden.

Ministers of religion . . . should not be used as comic characters or as villains.[4]

It is interesting that the code did not condemn violence in straightforward terms. So effective was the code that few producers attempted to resist it until the 1960s.

Similarly, the Roman Catholic Legion of Decency (founded in 1934) threatened to sponsor boycotts if it found films unsuitable for the viewing of the faithful ("Legion of Decency," *The Film Encyclopedia,* pp. 707-8). Until the 1960s Hollywood producers took the organization's rating system seriously, indeed.

After World War II, the nation's commitment to its Judeo-Christian traditions seemed, if anything, to be reinforced. Few doubted that God had blessed the allies' war efforts. And the material bounty that rained down on the country after the war reassured many Americans that God's hand remained upon their land.

America emerged from the war well-muscled. It had become the world's leading industrial and military power. And Americans felt their oats. They went on a spending spree, buying everything from washing machines to those long-coveted nylons. They wanted to pursue life heartily after the discipline and sacrifices of the war years. In the 1950s sociologist David Potter argued that the concept of plenty decisively shaped the psyches of Americans.[5] Americans were more materialistic than ever, as they rushed to keep up with those ubiquitous next door neighbors, the Joneses. Many white Americans believed that theirs was the finest society. Others, notably blacks, Chicanos, orientals, and poor whites wondered if they would ever participate in what was essentially a white middle class American Dream.

Then, unexpectedly, storm clouds gathered on the horizon. The

4. "Production Code," *The Film Encyclopedia,* ed. Ephraim Katz (New York: Perigee, 1979), p. 934.
5. David Potter, *People of Plenty: Economic Abundance and the American Character* (Chicago: U. of Chicago Press, 1954), p. 69.

United States, now the leader of Western democracies, found herself locked in a Cold War with her former ally, the Soviet Union. In 1950 the Cold War turned hot when United Nations troops attempted to withstand the assault against South Korea by the North Koreans and eventually by the Chinese. The Korean stalemate made Americans even more sensitive to the strength of world Communism, coming as it did in the wake of the communist takeover of China and President Harry Truman's laconic announcement on September 22, 1949, that the USSR had detonated an atomic explosion. Despite their economic well-being, a number of Americans were seized by genuine anxieties and fears.

As if to demonstrate that America was still a Judeo-Christian country as opposed to atheistic Red China and Russia, in 1954 the phrase "In God We Trust" became the country's official motto and the phrase "under God" was appended to the Pledge of Allegiance. The first of the prayer breakfasts was served in Washington, D.C., in the early 1950s. Governmental officials and other leaders invoked God's blessing upon the land as they breakfasted on bacon, eggs, and coffee. Evangelist Billy Graham, who had come to national attention during his Los Angeles Crusade of 1949, became known as the President's friend. He, Bishop Fulton Sheen, and Norman Vincent Peale were the nation's most respected religious leaders. Yet for some critics, the country's fascination with unspecific references to God was too much like a civil religion.

What was the faith of Americans? Was it as diffuse as the politicians' rhetoric implied? To judge by a 1952 Gallup poll, the American people professed traditional beliefs but perhaps with less actual grasp of those beliefs than before. Ninety-seven percent of the population affirmed a belief in God, whereas 85 percent of the population declared that the Bible was "the revealed Word of God." Many declared that Jesus Christ "was God" (75%). On the other hand, a good number of Americans could not identify the four gospels.[6] Clearly, though, in spite of their vagueness on some specifics, the mass of Americans were at least formally attached to their Judeo-Christian heritage.

In practice, Americans devoted large sums of money to religious buildings. They were also the principal pocketbook of Christian missions in the late 1940s, replacing Britain in that role. They attended the crusades of Billy Graham, the rallies of Torry Johnson's Youth For Christ, and the missions of the Joint Department of Evangelism of the

6. Jackson W. Carroll, Douglas W. Johnson, Martin Marty, *Religion in America, 1950–Present* (New York: Harper & Row, 1952), pp. 29, 33.

National Council of Churches. They bought inspirational and self-help books by Norman Vincent Peale, Rabbi Joshua Liebman, Monsignor Fulton J. Sheen, and Billy Graham on how to find peace with God and how to experience good emotional health.

The commitment of Americans to the life of the nation's churches seemed to grow stronger. From a human point of view, sociologists have tried to explain that phenomenon by describing it as a reflection of the post-war baby boom. Between 1948 and 1953 the number of babies in this country rose by almost 50 percent. A large number of the adults who become the parents of children after World War II wanted those children to receive a religious education. The Sunday school population grew remarkably in the wake of the baby boom: 1945, 24.5 million in Sunday school; 1952, nearly 30 million; and 1956, nearly 38.6 million. In turn, adults often associated themselves with the churches to which they brought their children. Or they sought church membership as a means to put down local roots, even if temporary, in a mobile society. For these reasons and others, the percentage of the American population that possessed church membership shot up: 1940—49 percent; 1950—57 percent; 1955—60.9 percent; 1956—62 percent; 1957—61 percent. (All statistics in the paragraph are from *Eerdman's Handbook to Christianity in America*, p. 430.)

In the 1950s the distinguished social commentator Will Herberg offered an explanation of the greater willingness many Americans had to identify themselves as either a Catholic, a Jew, or a Protestant. He linked the phenomenon to their desire to be good Americans. A person could take a stand for the American way of life by his affiliation with a church or synagogue. Moreover, such affiliations usually demanded little sacrifice, though they gave much social respectability (*Eerdman's Handbook to Christianity in America*, p. 430).

For others, the dynamic aspect of what some called the Post-War Awakening was the movement of the Spirit of God in evangelistic outreach. Youth For Christ had spread to hundreds of towns by the mid-1940s. Missionary agencies grew as well, enlisting recruits from Youth For Christ, Moody Bible Institute, Word of Life, Southern Baptist churches, and other ministries. By the mid-1950s, over half of the American-protestant missionary force came from evangelical agencies, not from the mainline denominations.

For many Christians, the conversions reported at U.C.L.A. and other universities by Campus Crusade staff members, or at large Youth For Christ rallies in Los Angeles, or at Billy Graham's crusades were not to be explained in terms other than that of the gracious work of God the Holy Spirit.

By 1958, however, several commentators began to speak of the Awakening as a movement of the past. The more skeptical wondered if an Awakening had really occurred.

With all of its flaws, however, and there were serious ones, as we shall see, the fifties represented a time when Americans pulled together for common goals, and Judeo Christian values continued to shape community standards. Television producer Garry Marshall explained why he placed his situation comedy "Happy Days" (first produced in the late-1970s) in the fifties:

> I couldn't figure out how I could do a realistic comedy about young people today and avoid drugs and avoid the sexual revolution, because I know they wouldn't put that on television. So I said, what's the use—it's not real, people are gonna watch it and say: "Baloney, that isn't life." Then it crossed my mind—how can I beat this? I can do it if I push it back in time—to the fifties. If I'm not doing drugs, and I'm not doing sex things, then the audience will buy it and they'll say: "That's right—it's not today, but that's the way it was."[7]

Marshall's intuition was brilliant. It is probably true that "Happy Days" is popular because it takes millions of Americans back to a decade less snarled in the merciless webs of drugs and free-lance sex, one that was more happy.

THE SIXTIES

It would be pointless for us to attempt to give an explanation of how American culture changed as it moved from the fifties, through the sixties and seventies, until our own day. The sophisticated cultural analysis that such an undertaking demands exceeds our capacities and knowledge.[8] Rather we shall provide a few impressionistic remarks that will have to suffice for the present discussion. We hope they will bring into sharper focus the problems Christians face in renewing their minds in modern America.

Few scholars today doubt that in the 1960s received values took a rude beating. The sixties began much the way the previous decade had ended, rather sedately. To be sure, the 1960 presidential campaign in which Americans elected John F. Kennedy as their first Roman Catholic

7. Cited in Rick Mitz, *The Great TV Sitcom Book* (New York: Richard Marek, 1980), p. 326.
8. For an attempt to analyze religion's role in contemporary society, see Mary Douglas and Steven M. Tipton, eds. *Religion and America: Spirituality in a Secular Age* (Boston: Beacon, 1983).

president provoked testy anti-Catholic rhetoric. But more generally, Kennedy's election represented a momentous breakthrough for Roman Catholics who thereafter competed in the American political arena on a more equal footing with Protestants. The Cuban missile crisis of 1962 transfixed the nation as the world stepped toward the precipice of nuclear war only to back away from it.

Then, on a fateful day in November 1963, as President Kennedy rode through the streets of Dallas, he was assassinated by Lee Harvey Oswald. The nation was stunned by the terrible news from Texas. It mourned the loss of its young Camelot and attempted to discover if Oswald, himself mortally wounded by Jack Ruby, had been involved in a larger conspiracy. But even with those events, few Americans could have predicted in 1964 that by the last years of the decade, national unity would reach its lowest ebb since 1861, the first year of the Civil War. Few could have foreseen that their nation would experience shocks so severe that some in politics and some among the clergy claimed its very existence was threatened.

After 1964 the decade turned tumultuous and violent. The flash of assassins' guns was seen again. In 1968, Robert Kennedy and Martin Luther King, two leaders of great stature, crumpled before life-snatching bullets. Before that, in the summer of 1965, massive violence erupted in America's major cities. The black population in the Watts section of Los Angeles exploded in a rampage of singularly destructive force, and other American cities, such as Detroit, Newark, and Chicago, experienced the rage of urban blacks who saw themselves as have nots in a white-dominated, callous society that seemed to care little about their welfare. Overseas, the war in Viet Nam, like a famished ogre, demanded larger helpings of men and matériel. In increasing numbers, American men and women found themselves in a strange green land waging a dirty war some doubted the nation actually wanted to win. The war had a brutalizing effect on many of those who served in it and upon the country. The debate over the legitimacy of the war split national public opinion and provoked mammoth demonstrations and protests.

The attitude of the courts towards Christianity began to trouble some church people. In the 1960s the Supreme Court permitted young men to claim exemption from military service even though their religious beliefs did not include conventional definitions of a Supreme Being (United States v. Seeger, 1965; Welsh v. United States, 1970). Long gone were the days (1931) when the court claimed, "We are a Christian people."

The Supreme Court made other rulings in the 1960s that bore directly on the practice of religion. It struck down compulsory prayer in the public schools (Engel v. Vitale, 1962): "It is no part of the business of government to compose official prayers to be recited as part of a religious program."[9] In the School District of Arlington Township v. Schempp (1963), the Court disallowed public Bible reading and the saying of the Lord's Prayer in public schools. In the 1960s some Christians believed that the courts were removing from the public sphere the final vestiges of the nation's attachment to its Christian heritage. Because the courts had not defined atheism as religious, proponents of atheism could propagate its tenets in public schools and state universities with relative impunity. Frustration began to build in many Christians who saw the rulings the courts were making as reflecting a continuing erosion of Christian influence in the country. They believed the courts were turning against Christianity. Other Christians reckoned that the courts had no other alternative than to make the rulings they did in a society where a Christian consensus apparently no longer existed.

The Women's Liberation Movement also prompted much debate among American Christians and in society at large. During World War II thousands of women worked in the nation's defense industries. After the conflict, returning men generally took over their jobs. Many women went back to their homes to nurture the babies they bore during the baby boom that followed the war and to care for their families. Nonetheless, 32 percent of all married women were employed outside the home by 1960.[10] They experienced a division of labor by sex that often relegated them to jobs offering low wages or to jobs in fields that had come to be thought of as women's work: the secretarial, nursing, and teaching professions. In the sixties many of their daughters protested vigorously against a male-dominated society in which women did housework for no pay or received inferior wages if they participated in the work force. The Redstockings Manifesto boldly set forth a radical analysis of the contemporary scene: "Women are an oppressed class. Our oppression is total, affecting every facet of our lives. . . . We identify the agents of our oppression as men. Male supremacy is the oldest, most basic form of domination. All other forms of oppression (Racism, capitalism, imperialism, etc.), are extensions of male supremacy."[11]

9. Cited in David Wells and John Woodbridge, eds., *The Evangelicals: What They Believe, Who They Are, Where They Are Changing* (Nashville: Abingdon, 1975), p. 230.
10. Karl N. Dengler, "Revolution Without Ideology: The Changing Place of Women in America," in *The American Past: A Social Record, 1607–Present,* ed. Erwin Unger, et al. (Waltham, Mass.: Xerox College Publishing, 1971), p. 401.
11. Cited in Gerda Lerner, "The Feminists: A Second Look," in *Annual Editions in American History,* '73-'74, *Vol. 2* (Guilford, Conn.: Duskin, 1973), p. 209.

Proponents of the Women's Liberation Movement urged women to fight for equal pay for equal work, to gain control over the reproductive processes through using the pill, and to reconsider the common view that the nuclear family was the optimum social unit.

For many Christian women the Women's Lib message was both appealing and unnerving. On the one hand, the justice of some of its criticisms could not be gainsaid. Women had frequently sacrificed their goals and dreams for the better good of their families. They did not receive fair wages. On the other hand, the demands of some of the more radical advocates seemed to contradict basic teachings of the Bible concerning the family, the headship of the man in the marital relationship, and human sexuality. Still, the impact of Women's Lib was so powerful that some women were ashamed if they remained homemakers and did not work outside the home. A good number of women sought a larger role in the leadership of the churches. Strident debates broke out, in the mainline denominations in particular, concerning the ordination of women.

As Americans lived out their lives in the 1960s, many noticed a growing permissiveness towards sexuality. A chorus of voices hailed the Sexual Revolution as a long-overdue attempt to throw off America's Puritan heritage. In his much-publicized Playboy Philosophy, Hugh Hefner preached a version of liberated sexual ethics. He argued that Americans were unhappy because they were repressed sexually, and he asserted that if they emulated the Playboy Philosophy, they would find personal liberation and happiness. Hefner's statement that many Americans were sexually repressed probably contained more than a grain of truth. But the cure he advocated was more pernicious than the ailment. Although Hefner's magazine, *Playboy,* was founded in the 1950s, it continued to reach homes, factories, and dormitories throughout the 1960s.

The revolt against the basic Christian teaching that sex should be restricted to marriage became especially evident after 1965. In 1965 in the San Francisco area, Jefferson Poland founded the Sexual Freedom League. The league's preamble read: "We believe that sexual expression, in whatever form agreed upon between consenting persons of either sex, should be considered as an inalienable human right."[12] Rock groups and entertainment stars assaulted traditional standards of Christian morality through their gestures, lyrics, and cinematographic presentations. Hollywood began to replace back-street B-movies of

12. As cited in Jack Lind, "The Sexual Freedom League," in *The Age of Protest,* ed. Walt Anderson (Pacific Palisades, Ca.: Goodyear, 1969), p. 184.

earlier times with expensive glossy productions in which graphic sex and unremitting violence became commonplace. Roger Corman's *The Wild Angels* (1966),[13] starring Peter Fonda and Nancy Sinatra, attacked straight society head-on. Heavenly Blues, the leader of a gang of bikers, lamented the death of one of his buddies: "Life never let him alone to do what he wanted to do; [everyone] wanted him to be good." Then Heavenly Blues tried to explain what motivated the gang: "We don't want nobody telling us what to do. We don't want nobody pushing us around. We want to be free. Free to ride without being hassled by the man; we want to . . . have a good time" (Cagin and Dray, *Hollywood Films*, p. 59). An ethic of goodness was being shucked in the name of unharnessed freedom. The Beach Party movies of the early sixties and the Beatles' record "I Want to Hold Your Hand" were already beginning to seem innocuous. The days celebrated in *American Graffiti* were ending, and innocence lost could never be regained. The broader public's tolerance and appetite for more explicit sex and violence was beginning to expand.

The attitude of the younger generation toward sexuality shifted in advance of their parents. Pollster Daniel Yankelovich noted that in 1969, 77 percent of college students believed extramarital sexual relations were morally wrong; in 1971, 57 percent; that in 1969, 42 percent of college students believed that relations between consenting homosexuals were morally wrong; in 1971, 25 percent; and that in 1969, 34 percent of college students believed that casual premarital sexual relations were morally wrong; in 1971, 25 percent. A sexual revolution appeared to be in full swing.

Polls in the 1960s indicated that an increasing number of Americans believed that religion was losing its influence: 1957, 14 percent of a Gallup sampling; 1962, 31 percent; 1965, 45 percent; 1967, 57 percent.[14] Until 1965 church membership in most Protestant denominations continued to grow. But from 1965 to 1975 leaders in several of the mainline churches saw their formal membership lists dwindle: the United Presbyterian Church, U.S.A. lost 12.4 percent; the United Methodist Church, 10.1 percent; the United Church of Christ, 12.2 percent; the Episcopal Church, 16.7 percent.[15] The decline in church attendance among Roman Catholics was equally startling. In 1963,

13. See Seth Cagin and Philip Dray, *Hollywood Films of the Seventies: Sex, Drugs, Violence, Rock 'n' Roll and Politics* (New York: Harper & Row, 1984), pp. 57-59.
14. Princeton Religion Research Center, *Religion in America, 1982* (Princeton: N.J.: 1982), p. 13.
15. *Erdman's Handbook to Christianity in America*, p. 464.

72 percent of American Catholics attended mass each week; in 1974, 50 percent. In 1971, only 41 percent of Catholics believed that absence from mass constituted a sin. Moreover, by the scores Roman Catholics simply ignored the Pope's encyclical *Humanae Vitae* (1968), which forbade the use of artifical birth control methods. To this day scholars debate whether or not Vatican II provoked unrest among the faithful; also, they ponder what caused the loss of membership in Protestant churches, save those that were conservative in theology.

In the sixties, then, Christians lived in a world in which many of their traditional values were publicly questioned or, what was worse, were ignored. Often they did not know how to respond to the rush of ethical change. Some prophesied that God's hand of judgment would smite the land if the nation did not repent of its sins. Others mused over the constitutional problem inherent in the Supreme Court's attempting to set moral standards for their fellow Americans. In addition, Christians themselves were not in complete accord concerning the nature of Christian values. Could a Christian be a capitalist? Could a Christian not be a capitalist? The place of Christian morality in American society seemed a far more complex issue than it had been just a few years earlier. During the period, received values, including Christian ones, took a beating. A good number of Christians reeled before the onslaught and were thrown off balance. And a good number of social commentators believed that the Puritan Epoch in American life had finally ended.[16]

THE SEVENTIES

The pathway of American religion has taken surprising turns. Few of those theologians who solemnly pronounced in the late 1960s that God was dead could have guessed how quickly He would be "resurrected" (He never died). As early as 1972, *U.S. News and World Report* published a volume entitled *The Religious Reawakening in America*. The book reviewed contemporary activities of the Jesus People, Catholic pentecostals, the practitioners of Eastern religions, and the occult. Religion, even the Christian religion, was once again newsworthy.

One of the most talked about manifestations of the Reawakening was the Jesus Movement. Belief in Jesus was "in." Enthusiastic converts who claimed His name were baptized in the Pacific Ocean, in streams, and in public fountains. Jesus Freaks took to the streets with

16. See, for example, Sydney Ahlstrom's *A Religious History of the American People* (1972; reprint, New York: Doubleday, 1975), 2:618-19. Ahlstrom discusses "the end of an epoch" in this work.

Bibles and tracts in hand, an experience-oriented gospel in their hearts, and a willingness to condemn sins. Christians plastered "Honk If You Love Jesus" bumper stickers on their cars and greeted each other with "One Way" gestures. Christian communes dotted the countryside from Texas to California. If a number of America's youth did not like establishment churches, they did love Jesus, and they sometimes portrayed Him as a radical or revolutionary. In the early 1970s, after the movement began to subside, Jesus People often enrolled in Christian colleges, bringing spiritual renewal to those campuses.

Besides the more flamboyant manifestations of a Christian youth movement, campus organizations such as Campus Crusade and Inter-Varsity called thousands of university and college students together for concerted reflection about the Christian faith. In the middle seventies a spate of books appeared describing what was called the Evangelical Resurgence. As a result of Jimmy Carter's election and George Gallup, Jr.'s, declaration that 1976 was the year of the evangelical, conservative Protestant Christianity had a national visibility it had not experienced for decades. Claims popped up regularly in the popular press that from 30 to 65 million Americans had been born again and were therefore evangelicals. George Gallup, Jr., whose polling studies received particular attention, used three criteria for sorting out an evangelical from the general populace: The person (1) had had a born-again experience; (2) "accepted the Bible as the actual word of God and interpreted it literally, word for word"; and (3) tried to encourage someone else to accept Jesus Christ as his or her Savior. Gallup reported in 1978 that 34 percent of the American population considered themselves to have been born again (including one in five Roman Catholics). He reported also that 61 percent of the Baptists affirmed that they had been born again, whereas only 11 percent of the Episcopalians did so. Half of those born again lived in the South, and 44 percent lived in small towns or rural areas. Twenty-three percent were non-whites.[17] Assuming that Gallup's poll was accurate, evangelical Christians constituted a sizable proportion of America's adult Protestants. For many Christians, the findings of the pollsters were reassuring. Perhaps there still remained a moral majority in the land.

The results of another type of polling were less reassuring. In *New Rules: Searching for Self-Fulfillment in a World Turned Upside Down* (see above), pollster Daniel Yankelovich charted the growing fascina-

17. George Gallup, Jr., *Religion in America* (Princeton, N.J.: Gallup Opinion Index, 1978), p. 45.

tion Americans had in the 1970s with the concept of self-fulfillment. His findings were often troubling indeed, from a Christian perspective.

Despite the much-ballyhooed discussion of changing values in the 1960s, the appeal of unfettered self-fulfillment was limited in that decade to college students, to proponents of the Women's Liberation Movement, and to members of diverse special-interest groups (Yankelovich, *New Rules,* p. 4). The majority of Americans still operated under the traditional rules regarding family, marriage, and the work ethic. Society told men that they were successful if they earned a good living, owned a comfortable home, raised healthy and well-adjusted children, and provided superior educational opportunities for their offspring. Society let women know that they were successful if they married, complemented their husbands as helpmates, and raised healthy and well-adjusted children. Society told parents that it was their lot to make personal sacrifices (duty to others) if they wished to win its recognition as successful people. Some Americans were happy as they went about their duties. Others were grim, convinced they were mere cogs in a big-business machine. In their opinion, the culture predetermined the way they were to live and to think with no regard for their individuality or their personal worth.

In the 1970s a sea-change in the rules of American society took place. Many Americans began to seek their personal self-fulfillment rather than accept the principle that they should sacrifice for others (Yankelovich, *New Rules,* pp. 10–11). Some even believed that self-fulfillment was their inalienable right in an affluent society.

As society's rules changed, success came to be defined as the pursuit of one's duty to self, not one's duty to others. A person was successful if he maximized his personal potential and enjoyment. If marriage, or children, or a mindless factory job stymied personal development, it should be forsaken. What was right became for many what made them feel good or what gave them satisfaction. Traditional notions of right and wrong based on a fixed ethic of the Judeo-Christian heritage were seen as outmoded. It was thought more pertinent to make distinctions between harmful and harmless. As long as an act was harmless to others, it was right; if it was harmful to others, it might be wrong. The gospel of self-fulfillment swept through American culture like a flood. Its evangelists ranged from pop songwriters to sophisticated and well-respected psychologists to the makers of jingles for commercials.

Nonetheless, according to Yankelovich's polling, 20 percent of Americans (34 million) remained basically unaffected by the change in the rules. They continued to operate under the old mores. As a result, although 17 percent of the population (29 million) built their lives "around norms that [made] a moral virtue of self-expression," the vast majority of Americans, 63 percent (more than 100 million), remained somewhere in between (Yankelovich, *New Rules,* p. 91). They applied the principles of self-fulfillment to select areas of their lives but worked under traditional values in other ones. Still, Yankelovich's pollsters discovered that by the late 1970s, 72 percent of Americans spent much time thinking "about themselves and their inner lives—this in a nation once notorious for its impatience with inwardness" (Yankelovich, *New Rules,* p. 5).

Yankelovich claimed that a probable correlation existed between widespread acceptance of the ideal of self-fulfillment and the more relaxed attitude toward divorce, the growth of tolerance for diverse kinds of social and sexual behavior, the changing perception of women in society, and the new evaluation of the work ethic. For example, society has become more indulgent toward someone who leaves a mate or family if that person can claim that he was unfulfilled in the relationship. Many came to see divorce as an almost inevitable outcome of marriage. Americans became more tolerant of those who sought fulfillment of their sexual drives outside of marriage. In 1967, 85 percent of Americans condemned premarital sex as morally wrong; in 1979, only 37 percent did. Acceptance of homosexuals increased as well. Some Americans turned the ideal of self-fulfillment into *carte blanche* for unchecked hedonism and self-indulgence. Attentive to society's messages about the good life, paradoxically they thought they were *obliged* to be sexually permissive and unfettered in their behavior.

There were positive changes, too. Americans began to appreciate more fully that a woman might reasonably choose the single life (Yankelovich, *New Rules,* p. 97). A profound change in societal rules had indeed occurred during the 1970s. Yet as pollster Yankelovich found out, there were scattered signs that a quest for an ethic of commitment was emerging.

The search for self-fulfillment stimulated in people a remarkable interest in themselves and provoked a wave of analysis by skilful commentators.[18] John Catoir noted that the fascination the self had for people was not always helpful in their nurturing a relationship with God. Writing in the *Catholic Digest,* Catoir astutely observed that "for too many people, their own satisfaction is of supreme importance to them. God is not in the place of highest honor. This kind of individual-

18. For a superb review of this literature, consult Ed Diener, "Subjective Well-Being," *Psychological Bulletin* 19, no. 3 (1984): 542-75.

istic thinking will usually subvert a relationship."[19] So pervasive was the fascination Americans had with themselves, that as early as 1976 Tom Wolfe described the period as the Me Decade and compared it to a third religious Awakening.[20]

Whereas Yankelovich argued in 1981 that the quest for self-fulfillment had redeeming features, in 1978 Christopher Lasch averred that the virulent narcissism associated with the quest fostered an "impoverishment of the psyche." In his searching analysis of American society, *Culture of Narcissism: American Life in an Age of Diminishing Expectations,*[21] Lasch mustered a dazzling array of concepts to explain the presence of narcissism in America. One of his theories has evoked particular attention. Lasch argued (pp. 52–60) that in earlier times the Protestant work ethic held in check the potential Americans had for narcissistic self-indulgence. When the work ethic became less powerful in American life, the culture moved toward narcissism. Capitalism had forced individuals to partake in active externally-oriented competition. Also, Christianity had called men and women to be other-directed, to direct attention toward God and toward their neighbors. But in the twentieth century, new psychologies replaced Christianity as explanatory vehicles for human behavior. Many of those psychologies advocated inward-directed self-realization and self-actualization programs and thereby poured fuel on narcissistic bonfires. Lasch's provocative analysis has become the subject of much debate.[22]

THE EIGHTIES

Whatever theories ultimately win out among scholars to explain how and why narcissism became prominent in American life, few will dispute its presence in America even today. Psychoanalyst Jeffery Satinover wrote: "Narcissism is a culture-wide syndrome. It's a hallmark of our age, in the 'Me Decade,'" and Anne David, professor of sociology at Miami University in Oxford, Ohio, put the matter bluntly: "Our culture promotes a type of pathological [disturbed] narcissism. . . .

19. Cited in George Gallup, Jr., and David Poling, *The Search for America's Faith* (Nashville: Abingdon, 1980), p. 47.
20. Tom Wolfe, "The 'Me-Decade' and the Third Great Awakening," *New York,* 23 August 1976, pp. 26–40. Wolfe's essay should be read with care.
21. New York: W. W. Norton, 1979.
22. For criticism of Lasch's study, see Bruce Mazlish, "American Narcissism," *Psychohistory Review* 10, nos. 3–4 (Spring–Summer 1982): 185–202; and Peter Homans, "Narcissism Viewed from the Perspective of the History and Psychology of Western Religion," *Journal of Religion* 62, no. 2 (April 1982): 186–91.

We have a lot of grown-up two-year-olds out there expecting to be happy 'now.' "[23] James Hitchock, professor of history at St. Louis University, declared:

> If the disease of solipsism is not the creation of the "self-fulfillment" prophets of the past two decades, they nonetheless have functioned rather like physicians prescribing sugar to diabetics. Rarely in history has there been so obvious a case of the cure being worse than the disease — or, more accurately, [of the cure being] a cause of the disease.[24]

And although writers for *Time* magazine declared in one breath that the Sexual Revolution was over, they asserted in another that "no sexual counterrevolution is under way. The sexual revolution has not been rebutted, [it has] merely [been] absorbed into the culture."[25] Some Americans are apparently becoming more conservative (is this the beginning of a We Decade about which some commentators have spoken?) because they have experienced the heartache of being enslaved to freedom. But their new-found conservatism in life-style is often pragmatic (many are fearful of herpes); apparently it is not based on a return to Judeo-Christian values.

Other Americans have not yet learned the lesson that unbounded indulgence brings about unbounded pain. Many people want to please themselves right now, not next week or next year. They have become addicted at the well of instant gratification. They cannot get enough of its poisoned waters. Every day inviting commercials beckon them back with familiar refrains: "You only go around once"; "Look out for number one"; "Grab the gusto"; "I love me." With the apparent collapse of Judeo-Christian community standards, there are few social restraints to hold Americans back from indulging their desires. Yet the frantic quest of individual Americans to create a sense of their own importance or to tie onto a lasting high is a futile one. They can never get enough. Their egos cannot be stroked sufficiently well, nor can their flesh be pandered to enough to give them satisfaction. They will only use up their own bodies, things, and other people as they rush pell-mell toward personal ruin.

Accompanying the Americans' fascination with self-fulfillment is their heightened concern for personal rights. Many Americans do not want to be told much, and they will try to get away with whatever they can. Such is the opinion of a federal judge who travels from one

---

23. Both quotations from *U.S.A. Today,* 7 July 1982, p. 3D.
24. "A Child of His Times," *National Review,* 19 March 1982, p. 300.
25. "The Revolution Is Over," *Time,* April 1984, p. 83.

jurisdiction to another. Based on the cases brought before him, he believes that a strong anti-authoritarian trend is developing in the country. Many Americans are unwilling to submit to the laws of the land or to the teachings of the churches and the schools if those contradict their own judgments or personal feelings. Such Americans believe that the quest for personal self-fulfillment should not be hampered by moral restrictions or inhibiting laws. In the name of personal freedom the homosexual community has launched a powerful crusade against those whom they see as attempting to disenfranchise its members of full participation in American society. In the name of personal freedom men and women have decided to abort unborn children who might be encumbrances to their lives. In the years since Rowe v. Wade (1973), 13 million unborn infants (4,000 every day at the present) have been put to death—a national tragedy that defies commentary.[26] By the scores Americans worship the god of personal freedom. They want to throw off any vestiges of a Judeo-Christian ethic that might restrain their life-styles, that might rain on their narcissistic parade. Their concerns are quite different from those of earlier Americans who struggled for personal rights in the context of an ultimate Lawgiver. But should they profess the Christian faith, there are a sufficient number of theologians in the academic community to ease their consciences by saying that homosexuality and abortion, for example, do not contravene the teachings of Holy Writ.

But what does this have to do with us as Christians? Are we not sheltered from the sins and enticements of the culture? No, not at all. As Christians, we are called by the Lord to live in the world but not be of it. Moreover, even if we profess that the Bible is our infallible rule of faith and practice, we are not beyond the reach of the charm of the gospel of self-fulfillment. We are, after all, sinner-saints. The gospel of self-fulfillment caters directly to our self-centered old nature. In a Me-Decade we may think that the teachings of Christ about self-denial, about losing one's life to find it, and about discipleship are fanatical, old-fashioned, or beside the point. We may show a high tolerance for the indulgence of the flesh, whether we encounter it in the viewing of television programs or encounter it close at hand. It is possible for us to strive to make our lives comfortable and to forget about the pain and wants of our neighbors. In the name of cheap grace it is possible for us to minimize biblical passages that speak of God's judgment of pride, sexual impurity, and covetousness.

Even if we sense that the gospel of self-fulfillment is only a tawdry

26. Christian Action Council, *The Least of These.* Pamphlet, Summer 1984.

counterfeit of the wonderful gospel of Jesus Christ, it is possible for us to accept more of the false gospel's values than we realize. Not that we disbelieve the Bible per se. We simply neglect its teachings about sexuality and about the value of a Spirit-controlled ego. The supreme commandment to love the Lord our God with all our heart, soul, and mind drops from our consciousness. We want to be good Christians, but the culture has infiltrated the way we think and live. The temptation to compartmentalize what we say we believe from what we actually do is almost irresistible. In a growing number of circumstances, we can cease to make the Bible our rule of faith and practice.

Rather than experiencing the abundant Christian life, we dutifully struggle with feelings of guilt and self-recrimination for our spiritual failures. We wonder why we suffer from such a shortage of spiritual power. We do not know where to turn.

By God's grace, millions of our brothers and sisters in Christ do mesh deeds with words even in this narcissistic age. They are salt-and-light Christians. They try to love their neighbors as themselves. They make sacrifices for their family members, for fellow Christians, and for the poor and sick. They seek their ultimate fulfillment in pleasing Christ, not in satisfying every personal whim. They enjoy the gifts of life but within the guidelines set by Scripture. They appreciate the wholesomeness of sexuality within marriage. They understand that material blessings are not to be hoarded but are to be shared with others. They marvel at the beauties of nature. They regard the splendors of a crimson sunset over the Arizona desert as the handiwork of the Creator. What is more, they experience spiritual power. But probably even they wrestle with the self-centered temptations of today more than their Christian brothers and sisters would guess.

How can the Christian tell if he is drifting toward an unhealthy fascination with self-fulfillment? His answers to the following questions may give him clues.

1. What is the ratio between the amount of time you devote to watching, listening to, or reading materials that contribute to your spiritual growth and the time you give to other fare? If the ratio favors non-Christian materials, you may be feeding the old nature and starving the new. The psalmist reminds us that the "blessed" man delights in the law of the Lord and "meditates day and night" on the law (Psalm 1:2).

2. Has your Christian faith ever cost you anything? If your faith has cost you nothing in recent months or years, are you actually bearing your cross daily and following Christ? Jesus said, "If anyone wishes to

come after Me, let him deny himself, and take up his cross, and follow Me. For whoever wishes to save his life shall lose it; but whoever loses his life for My sake shall find it" (Matt. 16:24-25).

3. Do you want to be a disciple of Christ, or does that idea strike you as being fanatical? Jesus said, "Not every one who says to Me, 'Lord, Lord,' will enter the kingdom of heaven; but he who does the will of My Father who is in heaven" (Matt. 7:21).

4. When you spend time with non-Christians, are you a different person from the one you are with people at church?

5. Have you felt guilty and hypocritical for weeks because you indulged in practices that you knew displeased the Lord?

6. Is your tolerance level so high you are hardly ever offended by anything you read, hear, or see?

7. How often do you call upon the Lord each day? Or do you rely upon yourself? Jesus said, "Apart from Me you can do nothing" (John 15:5).

8. Do you consciously seek to obey biblical teachings each day?

9. Do you love your heavenly Father and worship Him, or are you interested only in how He can meet your needs and desires?

We live in a society in which Christian churches do not exercise a decisive role in shaping public and private morality and policy.[27] Our culture is truly a secular one. All of us can profit from reflecting upon the critically important matter of renewing our minds in such a world. The massive onslaught of our culture against our minds forces us to do so. And then we must return to the basics: prayer, Scripture meditation, devotional Bible study, and a commitment to the local church and to each other. Moreover, we must relearn a lesson we may have understood well once before: on our own, we cannot win the battle for our minds; on our own, we cannot penetrate the culture with the gospel of Christ. We fight against spiritual powers that are unimpressed by wealthy churches, professions of orthodoxy from spiritually-cold hearts, and slick strategizing. Our strength comes from the Lord alone. He is our victory (John 15:5).

In *Megatrends: Ten New Directions Transforming Our Lives* John Naisbitt proposed that today the United States is "undergoing a revival in religious belief and church attendance."[28] Conservative Christians

---

27. For sophisticated discussions regarding the concept of secularization, see David Martin, *The Religious and the Secular: Studies in Secularization* (New York: Schocken, 1969); and David Martin, *A General Theory of Secularization* (Oxford: Blackwell, 1978). The literature by French scholars on secularization in France is immense.

28. Sixth edition (New York: Warner Brothers, 1984), p. 269.

have contributed greatly to that revival, according to Naisbitt. Let us keep that in mind. And then let us move forward. With the Holy Spirit's power to guard our minds, we can resist the attacks of the evil one. With the strength of the Holy Spirit, we can make advances for Christ's church in these days of vanishing securities but of unusual opportunities. With the strength of the Holy Spirit, our minds can be renewed. We can begin to develop "the mind of Christ."

2 Spiritual and Mental Health in the Balance

Paul Meier, M.D.

To prepare myself as a Christian psychiatrist, I undertook college studies, an M.S. degree in human physiology, an M.D. from medical school, psychiatric residency training in two different programs, and theological coursework from two evangelical seminaries. During those years of preparation, I was equipped with many techniques and short-cuts for bringing human beings relief from anxieties, depression, phobias, fears, insecurities, and other kinds of emotional and physical pain. Among the many tools I learned to use, by far the one that has been most valuable in helping people attain spiritual well-being is Scripture meditation.

Because man is a holistic being, his spiritual, psychological, and physical faculties are complexly intertwined. Every aspect of man's nature affects him as a whole being. Daily meditation on the principles of life passed on from man's loving Creator is more important for his health than food or sex or any other factor.

A primary reason Scripture meditation is vital for holistic health is that God's thought patterns and values are in sharp contrast to

Paul Meier (M.S., Michigan State University; M.D., University of Arkansas Medical Center; residency in psychiatry, Duke University and University of Arkansas Medical Center; M.A.B.S., Dallas Theological Seminary) is associate professor of pastoral ministries at Dallas Theological Seminary. He has written *Christian Child Rearing and Personality Development, Happiness Is a Choice,* and *Family Foundations.*

mankind's. Man is a totally depraved being, possessing selfish and ultimately self-destructive thought patterns and behavior. Show me a natural man, untaught in God's principles, and I'll show you a natural man who suffers from emotional pain. I'll show you a man who experiences the guilt and discomfort of a God-vacuum. I'll show you a man who is unconsciously fighting and struggling for a sense of significance, using worldly ways (e.g., sexual fantasy, materialism, power struggles, and prestige) in a vain attempt to attain significance, all of which will fail. The ways of the world bring temporary relief, like bandaids on open flesh wounds, but not ultimate relief from man's inner awareness of his insignificance apart from God. The billionaire John D. Rockefeller was once asked by a reporter how much money it would take to make him happy. Rockefeller scratched his chin and thought for a moment. Then he replied, "Just a little bit more!" Such is the relief from insignificance man finds in sexual affairs, power, money, or prestige. It only lasts for a little while.

Ultimately, man's sense of holistic well-being can come only from a personal relationship with God through Jesus Christ. But man needs more than salvation for joy and peace in his daily existence. Many of my anxious, depressed, and even suicidal patients are born-again believers who have not yet been taught how to appropriate personally God's thought patterns and behavioral principles, as outlined in the Bible. Instead, they have been misinformed by their parents, their peers, and frequently even by their churches. They have learned to think negative, self-critical, other-critical, destructive thoughts. They have become accustomed to behavior patterns that result in increased guilt, insecurity, and feelings of insignificance.

SEMINARIANS AND RENEWING THE MIND

A few years ago I conducted an extensive research study on seminary students from an evangelical seminary. The research included giving psychological tests using the Minnesota Multiphasic Personality Inventory (MMPI) and asking participants to fill out an extensive spiritual life questionnaire. The completed psychological test results were divided into three groups:

Group A: Those with exceptionally good mental health and a high level of maturity

Group B: Those with apparently normal mental health and maturity

Group C: Those with statistically significant psychological conflict and emotional pain

Then I ran statistical analyses comparing the level of mental health and maturity of each participant with his response to each factor on the spiritual life questionnaire.

When the results came in, initially I was surprised and disappointed. Those seminary students who had been Christians for many years were only slightly healthier and happier than those who had accepted Christ in the past one or two years. The difference was not even statistically significant. However, my disappointment turned to joy. I learned one of the most valuable lessons of my life when I found the factor that made the difference. That factor was Scripture meditation. Students who practiced almost daily Scripture meditation for *three years* or longer were significantly healthier and happier than students who did not meditate on Scripture daily. Also, they were significantly healthier and happier than students who had meditated on Scripture daily for *less than three years*. The level of significance on the various psychological scales varied from the 0.05 level (meaning only one chance in twenty that the correlation was a coincidence) to the 0.001 level (meaning only one chance in a thousand that the correlation was a coincidence).

What I learned from this research can be summarized as follows:

1. Even though trusting Christ is all that is needed to obtain eternal life, experiencing the abundant life Christ promised (John 10:10) and experiencing the fruit of the Spirit (love, joy, peace) rather than bitterness, depression, and anxiety are dependent upon a renewing of the mind.

2. Renewing of the mind can come from various sources, such as confrontation by loving friends about personal blind-spots, therapy with a Christian professional counselor, conviction from the Holy Spirit, confrontation with scriptural principles in sermons or seminars, and daily meditation on Scripture.

3. Renewing of the mind is a continual process, a progressive sanctification requiring continual, preferably daily, input from God's Word.

4. Daily meditation on Scripture, with personal application, is the most effective means of obtaining personal joy, peace, and emotional maturity.

5. On the average, it takes about three years of daily Scripture meditation to bring about enough change in a person's thought pat-

terns and behavior to produce statistically superior mental health and happiness.

6. None of the students in Group C (those with statistically significant psychological conflicts) were presently meditating on Scripture daily, although some were reading their Bibles regularly as a textbook for their classes.

7. All of the students who had meditated on Scripture daily, or almost daily, for three years or longer were in Group A or Group B, with most being in Group A (superior in mental health, happiness, and maturity).

A TROUBLED CHRISTIAN FINDS HELP

Mary D. was thirty years old. She was married to a loving Christian husband; had two children, both in good health; and was financially secure but not wealthy. She attended a good local church, where her husband was a church officer. There were no external circumstances in her life at the time that would have been likely to make Mary suicidally depressed. Her conflicts, like those of most humans, were within herself and stemmed from early childhood thought and behavior patterns.

Mary had been depressed off and on most of her life, but for several months Mary experienced increasing anxiety, depression, insomnia, loss of appetite, loss of sexual drive, loss of energy, early morning headaches, crying spells, feelings of hopelessness, infections, and a fear of losing her mind. She had absolutely no insight into what might be causing her psychological and physical symptoms. She hoped that her symptoms were caused by hypoglycemia or some hormonal deficiency because that would be less embarrassing than to admit to her friends that she had psychological conflicts. However, a thorough medical evaluation by her family physician turned up nothing. The physician recommended psychiatric consultation, which Mary took as an insult. Unwilling to search within herself, Mary grew progressively worse. One evening she suddenly lost touch with reality, thought her husband was plotting to kill her, and left her bed to get a knife to kill her husband in self-defense. Fortunately, he woke up and prevented her from killing him. He was shocked to find out that she now believed she was God and that he was the devil. She thought she heard both God and demons speaking to her in audible voices (auditory hallucinations). Her husband called their pastor, an experienced counselor, who with his wife came immediately to Mary's house. Together, the three of them, husband, pastor, and pastor's wife, persuaded Mary to meet me at the hospital. After committing herself to the hospital, Mary again became violent, condemned the nursing staff to hell, and had to be physically restrained by six nurses and aides.

I gave Mary moderate doses of a major antipsychotic medication. Within thirty-six hours Mary was over her psychosis, and the delusions or hallucinations (voices) had ceased, although she was depressed and frightened by the fact that she had almost killed her husband when she was in a psychotic state.

After regaining her sanity through the help of medication, Mary willingly began daily counseling. It soon became obvious that her problems stemmed from early childhood. She was the only daughter of a controlling, critical, insecure mother and a passive father. She had two younger brothers who seemed to have adjusted reasonably well. Because of a mechanism known as projection, described in Matt. 7:1-5, insecure mothers nearly always are most critical of the oldest daughter, and insecure fathers are frequently critical of the oldest son. When Mary was growing up, her mother was overly-critical of her, with the result that as an adult the daughter was filled constantly with self-critical messages. Mary's mother was legalistic and rigid; consequently, as an adult, Mary was filled continually with false guilt over minor things most people would ignore. Mary's mother did not tolerate Mary's expressing her anger or other feelings; as an adult, Mary continually repressed her emotions, denied her anger, and even felt guilty for having normal emotions. Mary's mother was overly restrictive of young Mary; as an adult, Mary was afraid to make independent decisions or to be assertive. At the same time, however, Mary was in many ways a wonderful person. She was kind and was thoughtful to her husband, children, and friends. Yet she had significant emotional pain and strong feelings of insignificance because of her negative thought patterns, legalistic false-guilt, overdependence on others to make her decisions, and fear of becoming aware of her repressed hostility toward her mother, whom on a conscious level she loved dearly. In the hospital the truth was revealed to Mary carefully, step-by-step. Showing her too much truth too quickly would have tipped her back into hearing "demon" voices and having paranoid delusions. Antipsychotic medications were continued to keep her brain's dopamine levels balanced to help prevent another psychosis. Mary's internal conflicts (spiritual and psychological) had also resulted in all of the physiological symptoms of depression (fatigue, insomnia, loss of appetite, loss of sex drive, and so on). Those symptoms only come when emotional conflicts are severe enough to cause depletion of serotonin and norepinephrine, two essential brain amines. Therefore, Mary was given antidepressant medications as well to speed up her physiological recovery.

As daily homework, Mary was asked to meditate on Scriptures related to her problems, such as passages dealing with self-worth (Ps. 139), legalism (Eph. 4:26), and unconscious vengeful attitudes (Rom. 12). Through meditation on Scripture and daily therapeutic confrontation with the truth about her resentment toward her mother, Mary was able to become aware of her intense but hidden bitterness toward her mother. She was then able for the first time in her life to forgive her mother. She was taught how her buried emotions and conflicts had resulted in biochemical changes in her brain, which in turn resulted in the depression and psychosis she had experienced. She was taught that though modern medicines could restore brain amines to normal quite rapidly, it would take right thinking, right attitudes, and right behavior to keep those brain amines normal in the future and to insure that she would not need medicine six months down the road. She was encouraged to meditate on Scripture daily to facilitate the renewing process. Also, she was encouraged to continue outpatient therapy for over a year to make sure she was not misinterpreting Scripture negatively and to give her continuing encouragement and support in her new ways of thinking. Within three weeks of hospitalization, Mary was over her psychosis and her depression. She continued to progress in outpatient therapy. Today she is living a happy, abundant Christian life and enjoying the fruit of the Spirit.

This true example—only the name and a few personal details were changed to protect confidentiality—illustrates the complex interweaving of the spiritual, emotional, and physiological aspects of man. Even Mary's infections were the result of emotional tension. Stress hormones in her body suppressed the white blood cells, which in turn resulted in fewer antibodies being produced, leaving her susceptible to physical illness.

Some well-intentioned but uninformed pastors might have tried to exorcise what seemed to be demons and blame her insanity (which would have been life-long if she had not got prompt treatment) on her lack of faith. Some para-medical quacks might have told her she had hypoglycemia or a nutritional disorder and then persuaded her to waste hundreds of dollars on megavitamins. Other well-intentioned but naive friends might have convinced her she had cancer and sent her to Mexico for laetrile treatment. Others might have blamed her problems on astrology. We live in a hysterical society today, one as riddled with native myths as were the Dark Ages. Only Mary's growing insight concerning her repressed feelings, coupled with meditation on God's inerrant Word, could have produced life-long joy, peace, and a sense of significance for this troubled Christian.

God's Perspective on Good Mental Health

When I was ten years old, my mother helped me to memorize Psalm 1. Psalm 1 teaches much about renewing our minds. Every Christian who is interested in good mental health as God perceives it should carefully reflect upon what each line of this psalm means for him or her in daily living:

> How blessed is the man who does not walk in the counsel
> of the wicked,
> Nor stand in the path of sinners,
> Nor sit in the seat of scoffers!
> But his delight is in the law of the Lord,
> And in His law he meditates day and night.
> And he will be like a tree firmly planted by streams of water,
> Which yields its fruit in its season,
> And its leaf does not wither;
> And in whatever he does, he prospers.
> The wicked are not so,
> But they are like chaff which the wind drives away.
> Therefore the wicked will not stand in the judgment,
> Nor sinners in the assembly of the righteous.
> For the Lord knows the way of the righteous,
> But the way of the wicked will perish.

The Psalm clearly teaches that there is a direct relationship between Scripture meditation and God-given happiness.

Some Recent Research on Meditation

Especially in the past twenty years, literally hundreds of research articles have demonstrated the close correlation between psychological stress and physical illnesses of nearly every kind. It is not the purpose of this chapter to give a lengthy summary of those problems. Rather it is to encourage the reader to improve his or her own existence and growth toward Christ-like maturity by learning more about meditation.

One of the most interesting secular studies on the value of meditation per se was conducted in 1974 by Herbert Benson, M.D., a professor at Harvard Medical School and a cardiologist. Dr. Benson published his findings in an article in the *Harvard Business Review,* July–August 1974, pp. 49–60, entitled "Your Innate Asset for Combating Stress." He chose the *Harvard Business Review* rather than a medical journal because he wanted to help overworked men and women reduce their stress levels and thereby prolong their lives and increase their enjoyment of life.

Dr. Benson described some of the physiologic changes that take place during stress, including elevated blood pressure. In our everyday lives, whenever we experience a stress that requires behavioral adjustment, our bodies respond with what Dr. Walter B. Cannon has labeled the fight-or-flight response. That response, Dr. Benson observed, "is characterized by coordinated increases in metabolism, oxygen consumption, blood pressure, heart rate, rate of breathing, amount of blood pumped by the heart, and amount of blood pumped to the skeletal muscles" (Benson, p. 50). It is mediated by epinephrine and norepinephrine (also called adrenalin and noradrenalin) and leads to coordinated activity by the sympathetic nervous system. The response helps us either to fight or to flee in situations we perceive as being potentially dangerous emotionally or physically.

Yet "although the fight-or-flight response is still a necessary and useful physiologic feature for survival, the stresses of today's society have led to its excessive elicitation" (Benson, p. 50). When the response is called upon so frequently, chronic high blood pressure occurs, which predisposes a person to heart attacks or to strokes, the cause of over 50 percent of all deaths each year in the United States. Dr. Benson estimates that from 15–33 percent of Americans, many of them business executives, suffer from varying degrees of high blood pressure.

Dr. Benson compared the physiological benefits of various types of meditation, including progressive relaxation, autogenic training, Zen, yoga, and transcendental meditation. He found that most of the meditation techniques were physiologically beneficial and counteracted the effect of the fight-or-flight response on such variables as oxygen consumption, respiratory rate, heart rate, blood pressure, and muscle tension. They also tended to increase brain alpha waves on the EEG. Dr. Benson proposed his own method of meditation, relaxation response, and observed that for any meditation technique to elicit beneficial physiological responses, it must have four basic elements:

1. A quiet environment (no noise or music)
2. A mental device (repeated thought on a single topic or word to free oneself from externally-oriented thoughts or worries)
3. A passive attitude (passively disregarding the distracting thoughts that tend to intrude on the mind, but not actively fighting them, because that often makes them worse)
4. A comfortable position (to reduce muscular effort to a minimum)

In October 1977, Dr. Benson was one of the guest lecturers at The Midwest Symposium on Meditation-Related Therapies held in St. Louis, Missouri. There he reported that after the publication of his article on meditating through relaxation response, Harvard psychiatrists as well had found the physiologically beneficial responses in Christians who prayed meditatively or who meditated on single principles or phrases from the Bible. Medical patients who had various degrees of high blood pressure were taught to meditate twice a day for twenty-five weeks. They experienced an average decrease of blood pressure of 8 mmHg systolic pressure and 5 mmHg diastolic pressure. The higher the patient's initial blood pressure, the greater the potential drop in blood pressure. The patients were using Benson's method of Christian meditation; in fact, Benson found that his religious patients followed most closely the relaxation techniques he advocated for lowering blood pressure.

Dr. Benson warned that meditating while lying prone does not work well. Too many people fall asleep. He recommended that a person sit in a comfortable chair. Also, he observed that the kneeling position works equally well if not better than other meditative positions. Patients who kneel find it easier to stay awake. He pointed out that it is no longer popular in our society to pray and meditate once or twice a day, as it was in past decades, and he suggested that that may be one reason hardening of the arteries is becoming an increasing problem for Americans at younger and younger ages.

A SUGGESTED METHOD FOR SCRIPTURE MEDITATION

The following is a method of Scripture meditation I recommend for my psychiatric patients and use myself.

1. Go to a quiet place. Occasionally vary the place by going out to a lake or stream in private.
2. Get in a comfortable position, but preferably do not lie down.
3. Relax your whole mind and body, including the various muscle groups.
4. Pray that the Holy Spirit will guide you into applicable truths as you read God's Word.
5. Read consecutively through the Bible, but do not place any legalistic guidelines on yourself (such as "four chapters a day").
6. When you come to a verse that stands out and offers you real comfort or confronts you with a needed change in behavior, stop

and meditate several minutes on that verse or even on a phrase within the verse.

7. As you meditate on that single principle from Scripture, think of ways you can appropriate the principle to your everyday behavior. Passively resist other unrelated thoughts and worries that intrude upon your mind.

If Christians meditated in such a manner for ten to thirty minutes morning and evening, they would probably experience

1. greater knowledge of Scripture
2. greater personal application of scriptural principles
3. greater understanding of who God is
4. lower blood pressure and other beneficial physiologic responses
5. longer life of usefulness for the Lord here on earth
6. greater ability to passively resist anxieties of the day even during nonmeditative time
7. greater awareness of unconscious truths about their blindspots as they become less afraid of the truth and their minds put up less resistance to the truth

Those are no small gains. With the power of the Holy Spirit prompting us, we can experience the renewing of our minds on a daily basis. Meditating upon God's Word in order to think God's thoughts after Him is the key.

> Finally, brethren, whatsoever things are true, whatsoever things are honest, whatsoever things are just, whatsoever things are pure, whatsoever things are lovely, whatsoever things are of good report; if there be any virtue, and if there be any praise, think [meditate] on these things.
>
> Those things, which ye have both learned, and received, and heard, and seen in me, do: and the God of peace shall be with you.
>
> The apostle Paul, A.D. 64
> (Philippians 4:8-9, KJV)

A Personal Confession

At the time I was carrying out my research on meditation, I came across Matthew 11:30. The verse profoundly affected me. Christ is calling men to be His disciples, and He concludes His call by saying (KJV),

> For my yoke is easy,
> and my burden is light.

For the next several days, I spent my meditation times reflecting on the implications of that verse in my own life and expressing my feelings about it to God. My first reaction to the passage was sarcastic laughter:

Who are you trying to fool, God!
I'm your disciple, and I am swamped night and day.
I'm teaching, writing, witnessing, counseling, speaking in public
   and carrying on a psychiatric practice! I'm worn out!
I don't even have time to relax or enjoy my family. Being your
   disciple is a heavy yoke and a heavy burden. Serving
   you has cost me a great deal personally!

The more I thought about it, the angrier I became at God for placing such great responsibilities on me and then having the nerve to write in His Word, "My yoke is easy, and my burden is light."

My initial sarcasm was followed by anger toward God. But when I continued to think about the passage, I realized that God cannot lie. If God says discipleship is a light, easy burden, then a workaholic discipleship experience must be out of God's will. The more I thought about it, the more God's Holy Spirit convinced me that I was operating partly out of love for God and partly out of a sense of legalism. Gradually I changed my whole life-style. I gave up many of my Christian activities and focused on the few that I was convinced were God's easy yoke. Also, I started spending more time with my wife, children, and friends. Since that time I have written over a dozen books and helped build the largest Christian psychiatric clinic in the world—all while working at a relaxed pace and enjoying the abundant life in Christ.

Slowing down helped me to accomplish more of what God wanted me to do. I could recount hundreds of other experiences I have had through Scripture meditation that have changed my life, step, by step, by step. But I don't have time, praise the Lord! I'm too busy enjoying my family!

I urge those who read this book to think God's thoughts and do God's work, at a reasonable pace, by meditating daily on God's precious thoughts. Read consecutively through the entire Bible, pausing to mull over passages that startle or particularly inspire you. Every time you read through the Bible, different passages will stand out, because God's Holy Spirit will already have accomplished His will in you from the passages that you meditated on and applied the first time through. May the principles of Scripture meditation revolutionize your life and enable you better to further the cause of Christ on earth until He returns.

Part 2
A Biblical Imperative in Renewing Our Minds

3 What Is Biblical Meditation?

Walter C. Kaiser, Jr.

The art and practice of meditation as defined by the Scriptures plays an important part in the development of the individual believer. Meditation is presented in Scripture as an act of worship involving divine communion. It results in such spiritual renewal and refreshment that the believer is thereby prepared to enter into the demands of life and the world as they are spread before all men. Rather than being an avenue of escape through which the individual is swallowed up, absorbed, or mingled with the divine in some unspecified mystical process, the meditation in Scripture, seen through careful definition of the objects, results, and the methods of the practice, is a spiritual exercise that preserves the identity, dignity, and value of the reflective worshiper. This essay will (1) define a biblical concept of meditation, (2) identify the biblical objects of meditation, (3) classify the types of meditation, and (4) comment on the significance of biblical meditation.

Walter C. Kaiser (B.A., Wheaton College; B.D., Wheaton Graduate School; M.A., Ph.D., Brandeis University) is academic dean and vice president of education, and professor of Old Testament and Semitic languages at Trinity Evangelical Divinity School. Dr. Kaiser has written *The Old Testament in Contemporary Preaching; Classical Evangelical Essays in Old Testament Interpretation; Toward an Old Testament Theology; Ecclesiastes: Total Life;* and *The Uses of the Old Testament in the New.*

DEFINITION

Several consecration formulas set forth the concept as well as any formal definition might.

> Let the words of my mouth
>   and the meditations of my heart
> be acceptable in your sight, O Lord ...
>
> (Ps. 19:14, WK)

> I will meditate on Your precepts
> and fix my eyes on Your ways.
>
> (Ps. 119:15, WK)

> Make me understand the way of Your precepts,
> And I will meditate on Your wonderous works.
>
> (Ps. 119:27, WK)

> May my meditation be pleasant to Him;
> I will be glad in the Lord.
>
> (Ps. 104:34, WK)

The Hebrew words used in these formulas represent basically two Hebrew terms. The more common of the two (appearing in the Bible in all meanings and forms about forty times) is hāgâh. Originally the term signified the cooing of doves (as illustrated in Isa. 59:11), but then it began to be associated with "reading in a soft voice," apparently because the soft murmur resembled the moan or cooing of doves. From there the idea appears to have passed over to one of reflection or meditation involving the murmuring individuals sometimes do when they are deep in thought. In the consecration formulas above, the root hāgâh also appears in the noun form in Psalm 19:14.

The other Hebrew root is śîaḥ. It too has been colored by a number of meanings, each with related nuances, and it is represented in the Bible by some thirty examples, most of them in Job and Psalms. The basic meaning of the word is to speak, to talk, to sing or even to lament or to complain. But when the word is used of talking with oneself, especially concerning divine things, it means to meditate or to muse. In this general setting it can also mean to pray to God or to commune with God.

In both of the Hebrew words the idea of conversation is closely related in vocabulary form with the concept of communication. When the ideas of conversation and of communion are linked to the consecration formula observed above, it is clear that meditation is at once a reflective act and conversation directed to God. Such meditation embraces not only the words of one's mouth, but also the thoughts of one's heart.

But before we enter into a more definite definition, we must notice that the New Testament also has a word meaning "meditate," the word *melataō*, which the Greek translation of the Old Testament used to translate the Hebrew term *hāgâh* (e.g., in Josh. 1:8; Ps. 1:2). In the New Testament, *melataō* appears in 1 Timothy 4:15 with the meaning of "to be careful," "to be diligent," "to take care," or "to practice" the things Paul has advised. The other New Testament word is *promeletaō*, "to meditate beforehand," or in the classical sense, "to prepare a speech in advance" (see Luke 21:14). The New Testament development of the root word was similar to the path of the Latin derivative *meditare*, which first meant "to reflect" and then meant "to exercise oneself in" or "to practice." Again the element of rehearsal, of forethought, and of the integration of thought into action appears.

Of course, the bare use of the technical terms for meditation cannot exhaust the scope or sources for the idea in Scripture. One need only observe the use of the concept in Philippians 4:8 (WK) to demonstrate that there were additional places in Scripture that called for reflective and meditative exercises.

> Whatever is true
> Whatever is honorable
> Whatever is right
> Whatever is pure
> Whatever is lovely
> Whatever is of good report
> if there be any excellence
> if there be anything worthy of praise
> meditate [or ponder; *logizesthe*] on these things.

Also, the Greek word *phroneō*, "to have this disposition of mind or mind set," in Colossians 3:2 and Philippians 2:5 is likewise worthy of consideration in a discussion of meditation.

A definition of the concept of meditation can be enhanced by examining the contexts in which these words are found, so as to make clearer what parts of the body are involved in meditation and what qualifications are imposed by the Scriptures on the act of meditation. When may one meditate? And how is meditation practiced?

The Scripture is explicit about the times for meditation. David confided that he thought of God when he went to bed and that he meditated on the living Lord throughout the night (Ps. 63:6). Such was his practice when he was in the wilderness of Judah fleeing from Saul, who was driven with a half-crazy jealousy over David's greater gifts of leadership. Likewise, an unnamed psalmist sings for joy and declares that his soul and tongue will meditate on God's righteous help "all the day long" (Ps. 71:23-24, WK). In a similar manner, Psalm 119:97 indicates that God's law has been the psalmist's meditation "all the day."

One psalm that can be classified as a meditation psalm because of the number of references in it to that reflective act of worship is Psalm 77. In three of its verses (3, 6, 12) there are references to meditating, with the word *śîaḥ* appearing in all three verses and the word *hāgâh* appearing in verse 12. The psalm falls into two parts: verses 1-9 express Asaph's sorrow and distress; verses 10-20 report how he rose above those problems. It was in a "day of [his] trouble" that the psalmist sought the Lord in a struggle of soul much like that of Jacob's wrestling with the angel (77:2). In spite of sleepless nights when he "called out aloud to God" (77:1, WK), he nevertheless "thought of God" and "moaned" and "meditated" (*śîah*) on Him (77:3, WK). He spoke mostly in silent thought and prayed in that kind of prayer where the mouth is silent, but the heart still prays in secret, much as Paul taught in Romans 8:26 that it is the Holy Spirit who in such sighs and moans makes intercession for believers with God.

In his disquietude, the psalmist tried to recall happier days in the past (77:5), and in the long hours of the night his song would return as he "communed with [his] heart," "meditated" (*śîah*), and his "spirit searched" and probed (77:6, WK). But such night recollections were also filled with tormenting questions: "Will God cast off forever? Will he be favorable no more? Has his lovingkindness come to an end forever? Have his promises failed? Has God forgotten to be gracious?" (77:7-9, WK).

Then a change of feelings came (77:10). The suddenness of that change has aroused much discussion. How is it to be explained? Most, like Gunkel, explain it psychologically. But surely the psalmist did not answer his own questions with an "impossible." Others, such as Weiser, suppose that an event interjected itself and gave the psalmist power to go on. But what was that event? No, the change must have been otherwise. It must have been in the object of memory and in the fact that the memory spoken of in vv. 1-9 led only to frustration, but the memory of God recharged the psalmist's energies and changed him. Before verse 10 the psalmist had been too subjective and had looked only within himself in attempting to determine the mystery of God's dealings. The psalmist was thinking solely in light of his own experiences. Accordingly, he experienced deep despondency. But when the psalmist's meditation (hāgâh) focused on the works of God, then he remembered that great deliverance of God experienced in the Exodus, which was a pledge of every other deliverance experienced by individuals or nations. Thus the text of the psalm emphasizes that it is a matter of great concern how one meditates and on what he fixes his heart and mind. Some meditation can be harmful, but biblically approved meditations strengthen.

Meditation is a function of the heart, to use biblical terminology. In Scripture the heart often stands for the whole person with all its functions, especially the mind. Such meditation of the heart is stressed in Psalm 19:14, Psalm 49:3, Proverbs 15:28, and Isaiah 33:18. In those passages thought is contrasted with spoken speech. In Psalm 49:3 (WK) the psalmist's "mouth speaks wisdom," but "understanding" comes from "the meditation of [his] heart." Likewise, in Psalm 19:14 the psalmist contrasts the "words of [his] mouth" with "the meditations of [his] heart." In both psalms meditation is seen as an inner reflection of one's mind and spirit. The point is made as well in Psalm 77:6 (WK) where "meditation" and the "search of [one's] spirit" are used in Hebrew parallelism to explain each other.

As such, biblical meditation is a rational process rather than a process of self-abnegation. The goal of meditation, according to Psalm 49:3, is understanding. Proverbs 15:28 (WK) asserts that "the heart of the righteous meditates [or ponders, hāgâh] how to answer, but the mouth of the wicked pours out evil things." If the art referred to in Psalm 49 and Proverbs 15 were the emptying of oneself so that the infinite could flow through one's being, then all acts of forethought, consideration, and reflection appearing in the Scriptures are wrong. But they are not. Biblical meditation is a rational, but whole-soul, experience. It springs from the heart and mind of the individual. It is spontaneous, yet most deliberate. The hard, sad events of life bring forth a spontaneous response and a desire to be with God. Yet there are times when the believer makes a deliberate decision of the heart to enter into song, prayer, or the worship of God. Psalm 77 illustrates the former, Psalm 119 the latter. But more on this later.

THE OBJECTS OF MEDITATION

No order of priority is assigned in the Scripture passages on meditation, but based on the sheer number of references, it would appear to be the clear contention of Scripture that Christian meditation has as its most basic object of focus the Word of God.

> This book of the law
> shall not depart out of your mouth
> but you shall meditate on it
> day and night.
>
> (Josh. 1:8, WK)

> Blessed is the man . . .
> [whose] delight is in the law of the Lord,
> and in His law he meditates
> day and night.
>
> (Ps. 1:1-2)

> I will meditate on Your precepts,
> and I will fix my eyes on Your paths.
>
> (Ps. 119:15, WK)

> Your servant will meditate on Your statutes.
>
> (Ps. 119:23, WK)

> I will meditate on Your statues.
>
> (Ps. 119:48, WK)

> I will meditate on Your precepts.
>
> (Ps. 119:78, WK)

> O how I love [Your] law!
> It is my meditation all the day.
>
> (Ps. 119:97, WK)

> I have more understanding than all my teachers,
> For Your testimonies are my meditation.
>
> (Ps. 119:99, WK)

> I will meditate on Your promises.
>
> (Ps. 119:148, WK)

It is clear that the mind of the meditator is not to be blank. Instead, it is to be filled with the inscriptured Word of God. Accordingly, the heart and mind had structure as well as content. Psalm 37:30-31 summarized the situation: "The law of his God is in his heart; his steps do not slip." But also "the mouth of the righteous ponders wisdom" (WK). The words of God must remain constantly in the believer's heart and be present in every situation he may find himself: when he sits down in his house, when he walks in the way, when he lies down, and when he rises in the morning (Deut. 6:6-9; Prov. 3:22-24; 6:22).

Biblical meditation was also on the varied works of God. As Psalm 77 made plain, to focus one's heart and mind on the greatest act of deliverance of all, that is, God's deliverance of Israel out of the land of Egypt (77:14-20), was to properly set the stage for realizing every subsequent deliverance in the life of any individual or nation. The psalmist exclaimed:

> I will meditate (*hāgâh*) on all Thy work,
> and ponder (*śîaḥ*) over Your mighty deeds.
>
> (Ps. 77:12, WK)

The almost identical words appear in Psalm 143:5 with the same two Hebrew words for meditation being used. In other similar passages, the reader was directed to ponder all God's works, only in those, the Hebrew word *śîaḥ* was used.

> Sing praises to Him;
> Meditate on his wonderous works.
> (Ps. 105:2, WK; see also 1 Chron. 16:9)

> I will meditate on Your wondrous works.
> (Ps. 119:27, WK)

> On Your wondrous works I will meditate.
> (Ps. 145:5, WK)

Without using one of the technical terms for meditation, Psalm 8 invited men to reflect on the works of God in creation and in His continuing operation of providence.

> When I look at Your heavens,
>   the work of Your fingers,
> The moon and the stars,
>   which You have established; . . .
> O Lord, our Lord,
>   How majestic is Your name in all the earth.
>
> (Ps. 8:3, 9, WK)

Thus the works of God, or as we would say today, His miracles, include His miraculous work in creation and each of His miraculous interventions in the course of the history of salvation.

The highest object of meditation was none less than the living Lord Himself. The psalmist exalted:

> I think of You on my bed,
> and meditate on You in the night watches.
>
> (Ps. 63:6, WK)

> My meditation of Him will be sweet;
> I will be glad in the Lord.
>
> (Ps. 104:34)

> I will remember Your name in the night, O Lord,
> and keep Your law.
>
> (Ps. 119:55, WK)

> On the glorious splendor of Your majesty,
> ... I will meditate.
>
> (Ps. 145:5)

In a similar vein, Paul counseled the church to set its mind "on the things above, not on the things that are on earth" (Col. 3:2). The things above, of course, are represented supremely in Christ and in all that is associated with the Godhead. Yet Paul did not refer to an other-worldly attitude that assumed a gnostic stance to the current world scene, for later he was to direct believers to fill their minds with those things that met the six ethical tests of Philippians 4:8, starting with what is true. Of course, the list in Philippians was not used as a basis for worship and communion with God, and therein appears the difference. Nevertheless, each of the ethical tests flowed out of a mind-set that considered first the mind that was in Christ (Phil. 2:5–8).

Interestingly enough, in Job, Eliphaz laid a similar spiritual condition on all who would properly enter into "meditation before God." He cautioned Job that he was "doing away with the fear of God and [thereby] hindering meditation (*síhah*) before God" (Job 15:4). Eliphaz's warning certainly was in the spirit of all scriptural teaching on meditation. It must begin in the "fear of the Lord," which may properly be considered an attitude of belief and trust and a willingness to hold to the view that he who comes to God must believe that he is there and that he is a rewarder of all who diligently seek him (see Heb. 11:6).

CLASSIFYING TYPES OF MEDITATION

Rather than attempting to classify texts of Scripture into the standard divisions of discursive meditation (where the person meditating goes from premises to conclusions in a series of logical steps) or intuitive or transcendental meditation (where the individual has immediate apprehension and knowledge without the conscious use of reasoning) we would prefer to develop another set of descriptive terms. It is obvious that where the intuitive or transcendental bypasses the specified objects of meditation as noted already, we would disallow it and prefer a more discursive type. Likewise, those terms which would emphasize whether or not the act of meditation was initiated by an act of the will (deliberate meditation) or was thrust upon one by the events of life (spontaneous meditation) are, likewise, not especially functional for most biblical data.

Instead we like to suggest that there are four categories of meditation: (1) reflective meditation, (2) commemorative meditation, (3) instructional meditation, and (4) worshipful meditation.

REFLECTIVE MEDITATION

In the first recorded act of meditation in the Bible, "Isaac went out in the field to meditate (*sîah*) at the evening time" only to be interrupted by the arrival of his bride, Rebekah (Gen. 24:63, WK). What the content or purpose of his meditation was is not mentioned. We may only guess. It may well have been that he merely wished to be alone with his thoughts and to muse and reflect over plans and decisions he had to make.

Similarly, Jacob mused over and pondered the implications of his son's bizarre dreams. "His father kept in mind" (*šāmar ʾet haddābār*) the question he had asked Joseph: "Shall I and your mother and your brothers indeed come to bow ourselves to the ground in front of you?" (Gen. 37:10–11, WK).

One could also point to Daniel 7:28 (WK), for although Daniel's thoughts so troubled him after he had received the magnificent prophecy of the conquest of the kingdom of God over the successive kingdoms of men that the very color of his skin changed, still "he kept the matter in mind" (*milletā*). Again, his keeping "the matter in mind" appears to be nothing more than a reflective type of musing and a considerate inspection of the known details of a matter, only those details are now being tossed about the mind with a view to draining them dry for possible implications and significances.

Finally, one must place Mary's contemplation in the same category. "Mary kept all these things [the message of the shepherds] and pondered (*sumballō*) them in her heart" (Luke 2:19, KJV). Later, when the twelve-year-old Jesus startled his parents with the announcement: "Did they not know that I must be in my father's house?" Mary again "kept (*dietērei*) all these sayings in her heart" (Luke 2:51, KJV). Thus the object of this type of meditation over words is only to realize the profound significance contained in the words. It is understood that only subsequent events will reveal all the implications that are contained in each statement.

COMMEMORATIVE MEDITATION

It was Jesus who exhorted his followers to contemplate the events of history and the examples it provides. In Luke 17:32, Jesus said, "Remember Lot's wife." So in 2 Timothy 2:8 Paul advised Timothy to "remember Jesus Christ risen from the dead, descended from David as preached by my gospel" (WK.; cf. 2 Cor. 4:14–18). Here the meditation is for the specific purpose that such thought should result in appropriate action.

The best illustration of commemorative meditation is given in 1 Corinthians 11:25 (WK). There, in connection with the cup of the Lord's Supper, the invitation was, "This do, as often as you drink of it, in remembrance of Me." The act of memory was not only to be reflective, but it was to be connected with an appropriate action that was embraced in the idea of remembering. The scope of this Semitic concept to remember involved both cognition and volition. Thus, for example when God "remembered" Hannah (1 Sam. 1:19), He not only called to mind her sorrowful state of barrenness but simultaneously acted on her behalf so that she became pregnant. So it would appear the followers of Christ must do if they are to properly memorialize His death and resurrection in the Lord's Supper.

INSTRUCTIONAL MEDITATION

Often the contemplation of the works of God, the law of God, and the Person of the Lord leads to further knowledge. The psalmist exults:

O how I love Your law!
It is my meditation all the day.
Your commandments make me wiser than my enemies,

For it is ever with me.
I have more understanding than all my teachers,
   For Your testimonies are my meditation.
I understand more than the aged,
   For I have kept Your precepts.

                       (Ps. 119:97-100, WK)

Such a person is described in James 1:25 (WK), "looking into the perfect law, the law of liberty." When he looks he does not forget but acts. James says that such a one shall "be blessed in his doing."

Not only is one promised growth in the knowledge of God, but success is also promised to Joshua for meditating on the law of the Lord day and night: "Then you shall make your way prosperous" (Josh. 1:8, WK). Consequently, the instruction is both preceptual and practical. In the latter case it will prepare one for life. The man who seriously meditates on God's law day and night is called the "blessed man" in Psalm 1:1-2. Together, both theoretical enlightenment and practical application are legitimate goals and are the results of one type of biblical meditation.

WORSHIPFUL MEDITATION

There is a kind of meditation in which one lingers in the presence of God for no other reason than to adore, praise, and enjoy the power, presence, and Person of the living God. Foremost among the expressions of this sentiment is Psalm 104:34 (WK):

      My meditation of Him will be sweet;
      I will be glad in the Lord.

Such delight comes from the steady look at the God we love and is described by the psalmist as enough to make one's "soul fat" and "to open one's mouth with praise to God" (Ps. 63:5-6, WK). The security of such closeness is graphically depicted in Psalm 63:7 as being one of resting "in the shadow of [God's] wings." There the psalmist "clings" to God, and God's right hand upholds him.

In Jeremiah 17:7-10 (WK), a passage similar to Psalm 1:2 describes the devout man, who, when he meditates on God's law, is like a tree that flourishes regardless of the outward circumstances. However, the focus of the description in Jeremiah is on the vital, ever-expanding root system, not on the foliage that is immediately apparent.

> Blessed is the man who trusts in the Lord
>   whose trust is the Lord
> He shall be like a tree planted by the water
>   that sends out its roots by the stream.

And as if to locate the sphere in which this trust originates as being the same as that of the man who meditated on God's Word, Jeremiah went on to say,

> I the Lord search the mind
>   and try the heart,
> To give to every man
>   according to his ways
>   and according to the fruit of his doings.

Such trust in the Lord and spiritual hunger for His Person is reflected in many other passages, even in those passages where the word for meditation does not appear. Two celebrated examples are these:

> As a deer pants after the water-brooks,
>   So longs my soul after You, O God.
> My soul is athirst for God,
>   for the Living God.
>   (Ps. 42:1-2, WK)

> With open mouth I panted,
>   For I longed for Your commandments;
> Turn to me and be gracious to me,
>   As You used to do to those that love Your name.
>   (Ps. 119:131-32, WK)

The heart of meditation is the sheer enjoyment of the presence of the living Lord and the delight that comes in praising His name. The goal of this type of meditation is reached when the worshiper has found the One whom his soul adores above all others.

> The Lord is good to those that wait for Him
>   To the soul that seeks Him.
>   (Lam. 3:25, WK)

That is worshipful meditation and communion with God.

Significance of Biblical Meditation

To what point does biblical meditation lead? Is its goal some kind of striving after totality, or is it action-oriented? Are there stages of meditation, for example, a movement from meditation to contemplation? And can the end of all worshipful meditation be union with God, or does such talk imply an unhealthy kind of mysticism for which pantheistic mysticism in the West or Buddhism in the East is well known?

In 1926, J. Pedersen noted that the Hebrew verb "to remember" (a concept frequently associated with meditating) often appeared in parallelism with "to think." In Pedersen's judgment,

> when the soul remembers something, it does not mean that it has an objective memory image of some thing or event, but that this image is called forth in the soul and assists in determining its direction, its action.... The peculiarity about the Israelite is that he cannot at all imagine memory, unless at the same time an effect on the totality and its direction of will is taken for granted.
>
> *(Israel: Its Life and Culture,* 2 vols., pp. 106-7)

Again he affirms (p. 123) that

> the very language shows how Israelite thought is dominated by two things: *striving after totality* and *movement.* Properly speaking, it only expresses that the whole soul takes part in the thinking and creates out of its own essence. The thought is charged with the feeling of the soul and the striving of its will after action.

However, if, as Pedersen contends, Hebrew thought (or as we are considering it here, meditation) and action are considered as a unit, then James Barr's devastating attack on this theory in his book the *Semantics of Biblical Language* (Oxford, 1961) must be allowed to settle the issue. For indeed, the two processes signified in the ideas of "to think" and "to act" can be distinguished in Hebrew mentality. The fact that the Hebrew word "remember" and similar related linguistic notions can denote a process of thought as well as an action is established on the basis of context and usage, but that does not necessitate an argument in favor of a special kind of Hebrew primitive prelogical mentality in which action is understood as "manifestations of the whole of the soul" (Pedersen, *Israel: Its Life and Culture,* p. 128). Pedersen himself (p. 128) says that for the Israelite—as for primitive peoples generally—the mental processes are not successive, but united in one, because the soul is always a unit, acting in one. But no more are the action and result to be distinguished from each other or from the mental activities; they are implied in the actual mental process. This is to be attributed to the fact that the soul is wholly present in all its works. The actions are not sent away from the soul, they are the outer manifestations of the whole of the soul, the traces of its movements: its "ways" the Hebrew calls them.

Barr is justified in his rejection of Pedersen's attempt to develop a theory of the "primitive" character of the Hebrew language. Not only is Pedersen's psychology highly debatable, but as Brevard Childs argued (*Memory and Tradition in Israel,* London, 1962, pp. 17–30), the "Hebrews were aware that thoughts do not always lead to a corresponding action" (p. 29).

However, without developing a theory about primitive mentalities or importing a so-called foreign category, such as prelogical thought, to Scripture, it is possible to say that biblical meditation was more than a stationary something with quiescent overtones. One often meditated on the law, on God's deeds in the past, or on His Person in order to move to legitimate action, as in the case of Joshua. Joshua's ability to lead his nation successfully was linked directly to his meditating on the law of the Lord day and night (Josh. 1:8). Thus meditation may be action-oriented but there is no semantical definition that requires that it be.

One may ask, "Are there not stages in the art and practice of meditation?" According to William Burt Pope (*A Compendium of Christian Theology* [New York: Phillips and Hunt, 1880], 3:230), there are two stages in devotional ethics:

> *Meditation* is the silent pondering of the soul on Divine things through the medium of the Word, the devout consideration of some particular truth, or revelation, or promise: as preceding, accompanying, and following all prayer it is the strength and best grace of devotion.
>
> *Contemplation* is the same posture of the devout mind, but with some exclusive reference to God Himself. It expresses the highest aim of the soul to behold the Supreme in anticipation of the eternal Vision.

In Pope's view, contemplation is the higher of the two stages and is the final goal of all true Christian devotion. It is "the state of detachment from every creature and the pure beholding of God alone as the only Being" (Pope, p. 230). Pope does not see Scripture as discouraging such an ambition, though he insists that as a safeguard "all contemplation be combined with prayer" (Pope, p. 230). One might add as well that contemplation should be further safeguarded by being rooted in the Scriptures and in the God who revealed Himself in Jesus Christ.

Pope clearly warns (p. 230) that

> the error of false Mysticism is to believe that the soul may be raised into a state in which every affection of the heart is stilled and all emotion lost in the fixed and unchangeable vision of Him in whom all desire of personal blessedness is forgotten.

Therefore, if there are stages in worshipful meditation (and we are willing to grant this may well be the case even though biblical revelation does not demand it), then Pope has given the best description of them. One needs only to insist on the safeguards already noted to assure that this meditation is the biblical variety and is not a watered-down imitation.

One final point of significance must be treated: Union with God. Again the subject is somewhat ambiguous, for union with the infinite has been a watchword in many systems of Eastern and Western Mysticism. But, as Pope cautioned (p. 231),

> the Union of which we speak is one that preserves inviolate the personal identity of him who attains it: he becomes *one with God* in thought and feeling and will: the emphasis being laid on the will.

Indeed in the Lord's final words to His disciples in the upper room discourse of John 17:21, He prayed that "they all may be one," and then He described the unity He had in mind in terms such as that enjoyed by the triune Godhead. In John 17, of course, the anticipated unity was not expressly linked with meditation. But the passage can be used to demonstrate that such union is not antithetical to the interests of Scripture.

Naturally, in biblical terms, union begins not with the act of meditation but with the new birth of Christ. But subsequently, that life can be nurtured as the believer worships God and meditates on His law day and night. Only then does he walk in the light as He is in the light, and only then does he have fellowship with the Light of lights. Yes,

> Let the words of our mouths
> and the meditation of our hearts
> Be acceptable in Your sight, O Lord.
> (Ps. 19:14, WK)

4 Mind Control or Spirit-Controlled Minds?

Grant Osborne

George Orwell's novel *Nineteen Eighty-four* recounts the story of a society in which Big Brother seeks to control the minds and actions of every citizen. Does this once futuristic novel describe society today? Although in the United States there is obviously no totalitarian government or rigid censorship, it can be argued that the media and advertising people are effectively controlling the decision-making of many people. Presidential elections, financial choices, and life-style preferences are all much influenced by media campaigns. Experts on persuasion say that media techniques have grown so sophisticated that those who master them can manipulate the masses in any way they wish. Mind control may be closer than is often realized.

How can a believer hope to gain control over his mind in a world such as this? Is it realistic any longer to seek to bring every thought captive to Christ when the material coming into one's mind from secular sources is like a daily blitzkrieg? Those are not idle questions. It is usually the mind where the deep spiritual struggles take place. Moreover, that which runs through a person's mind sometimes more accurately reflects who he is more than who he says he is. Proverbs 23:7 says of a person, "For as he thinks within himself, so he is."

Because the mind is so important in a person's spiritual life, it is

Grant Osborne (B.A., Fort Wayne Bible College; M.A., Trinity Evangelical Divinity School; Ph.D., University of Aberdeen, Scotland) is associate professor of New Testament at Trinity Evangelical Divinity School.

essential that one learns what the Bible has to say about it. Believers need to know how the Holy Spirit can renew their minds on a daily basis. Sinful deeds are likely to be preceded by sinful thoughts; without a Spirit-controlled mind, it is impossible to withstand the wiles of the Evil One.

The expression "renewing the mind" (see Rom. 12:2; Eph. 4:23) summarizes well what happens when a person's mind is transformed by the Holy Spirit. It links spiritual regeneration to ethics. God touches the mind in order to enable people he has acquitted (declared righteous, the judicial side) to perform good deeds (made righteous, an ethical result). Those who learn to control their minds, to becomes "doers" as well as "hearers" (James 1:22), will be blessed of God. Ethics has a more important place in the Scriptures than many Christians have acknowledged in the last few decades. Spiritual regeneration should result in a life-style and in deeds that are pleasing to God.

There are at least fifteen different words or word groups in Scripture detailing the place of the mind in the spiritual life. They range from the obvious ones, such as *think, understand, discern, perceive, suppose, conscience, will, remember, meditate,* or *know;* to concepts not often associated with the mind, such as *hear, see, inner man, test,* and *heart.* The last word, *heart,* is an especially prominent concept. Hans Walter Wolff argues that the heart is the seat of rational as well as emotional decisions.[1] He sees it as the center of understanding and decision-making (see 1 Kings 3:9–12), the place where the will operates (Ex. 36:2). The heart can properly be described as the whole person involved in gaining knowledge and moving to the point of decision. In the heart one meets God and turns to Him in worship and righteous deeds (cf. Ps. 51:10; 1 Sam. 12:24; Isa. 51:7; Jer. 12:3).

In both Testaments one cannot truly hear the Word of God without obeying it. The prophets introduced their message with the words, "Hear, O Israel," and a major injunction of Jesus was the statement, "The one who has ears to hear, let him hear." He commanded men to link what they thought and did to the revealed will of God.

The word *knowing* in Scripture has similar connotations. From the divine perspective, knowing refers to God's electing or choosing His special people (Num. 16:5; Jer. 1:5; Amos 3:2); from the human perspective it refers to the response of men to and their involvement in

---

1. *Anthropology of the Old Testament* (London: SCM, 1974). He says, "In by far the greatest number of cases it is intellectual, rational functions that are ascribed to the heart" (p. 46). In addition to Wolff, see T. Song, "Heart," *New International Dictionary of New Testament Theology* (hereafter, NIDNTT), 2:181; and Eichrodt, *Theology of the Old Testament* (Philadelphia: Westminster, 1967), 2:143.

(by way of obedience) His will, as in, for example, their support of justice (Hos. 4:1-6; Jer. 22:15-17). In short, in the Old Testament and in the New, renewing the mind brings about spiritual transformation at the deepest level of a person's being.

Ephesians 4:17-24 summarizes well the Bible's teaching on the subject. Let us take an extended look at the passage. It occurs immediately after the statement in verses 7-16 of Paul's philosophy of ministry. In that statement, Paul asserted that the leaders of the church were first taken captive by God (v. 8) and then were given to the church (v. 11) to teach and equip the saints so that they might minister to one another and to society (v. 12). As the church grew to maturity in Christ (v. 13) it would have to recognize the dangers confronting the weak, immature members (v. 14) and to unite in love, with all doing their part (vv. 15-16). The means by which that grave responsibility was to be fulfilled was spelled out in verses 17-24.

MIND CONTROL, EPHESIANS 4:17-19

PRECONVERSION:

In the first half of the passage, Ephesians 4:17-19, Paul delineated the biblical place of the mind in the spiritual warfare between sin and salvation. He described the conduct of unbelieving Gentiles in strong language meant to demonstrate the secular pressures upon the church. His description did not merely depict the non-Christian; at a deeper level it pictured the forces trying to shape the church, to "squeeze [it] into its own mold" (Rom. 12:2; Phillips). That Paul's reference was to Christians as well as nonbelievers can be seen in the words "no longer" (vv. 14, 17). No longer should believers continue in the practices that characterized their lives before they came to Christ. Paul warned the Ephesian Christians not to become helpless before the "deceitful scheming" of "cunning" men (4:14). The solemn introduction in verse 17, "I say, therefore, and testify in the Lord,"[2] highlighted the seriousness of the statement.

The place of the mind in the preconversion state can be seen in each of the phrases in of 4:17-18.

1. The expression "futility of their thinking" (v. 17, NIV) describes the vanity and emptiness of unbelievers' thought-patterns. Marcus Barth, *Ephesians,* Anchor Bible (Garden City, New York: Doubleday,

---

2. From *The New King James Version.* Copyright © 1979, 1980, 1982, Thomas Nelson, Inc., Publishers.

1974), 2:499, says of the term futility, "With one single word Paul describes the majority of the inhabitants of the Greco-Roman empire, including the shapers and beneficiaries of its magnificent cultural elements, as aiming with silly methods at a meaningless goal." In the twentieth century, atheistic existentialists such as Sartre and Camus have spoken candidly of the absurdity or meaningless of life, as if God did not exist. It does not take long to find other illustrations of the mindlessness of modern life. Television executives say they pitch their shows at the twelve-year-old; not surprisingly, the top ten television shows are frequently a study in futility. Yet those programs are shaping the mores and attitudes of the future.

2. The pagans are also described as being "darkened in their understanding" (v. 18), a phrase typifying the control of unbelievers' minds by evil. The expression may well refer to the "powers . . . of . . . darkness" (Eph. 6:12).[3] The mind is under assault by cosmic forces trying to subvert it to their will. The primary meaning, however, is that the mind of the secular person dwells in the realm of darkness, or sin. His understanding is darkened. That blindness is evident in many ways. It is amazing how a major television network can blithely label the strategy of those in favor of prayer in school as power politics while ignoring the hard-fisted tactics of the pro-abortion or gay rights movements. It is even more astounding that medical doctors who casually abort unborn babies will actually discuss the rights of two embryos and say, "The system does everything in its power to protect life." One wonders how so-called experts can pretend to be objective in light of their blatant attempts at manipulating public opinion.

3. Non-believers are referred to as being "separated from the life of God" (Eph. 4:18, NIV) The two reasons given in support of that assessment summarize the power of sin to control the mind. First is the statement "the ignorance that is in them" (v. 18, NIV). Intellectual misunderstanding is not in view, but rather the deliberate rejection of the way to God, a volitional act. In one of his monologues, Bill Cosby claimed that children are "brain-damaged" because whenever they are faced with a deliberate act of disobedience they claim, "I don't know why I did it!" (ABC, "20/20," 31 May 1984). The children's claim typifies the ignorance of the natural man. Second is the statement, "the hardness of their heart" (v. 18). Hardness of heart is behind ignorance of and rejection of God. The phrase is most commonly known as being

---

3. It is well-known that the spiritual warfare between God and Satan is a major, and characteristic, emphasis of Ephesians and Colossians. Some go so far as to consider it one of the distinctives of those epistles.

used of Pharaoh, but it is utilized elsewhere in the Bible to describe one who refuses to obey God. W. Mundle speaks of the repeated use of Isaiah 6:9-10 in the New Testament to describe God's "sentence of hardening" upon those (especially Israel) who hardened themselves to His call (see, for example, Mark 4:12; and parallels, John 12:40; Acts 28:27; Rom. 11:8) ("Hear," *NIDNTT,* 2:177-78). The concept of hardening focuses on the volitional side of man and notes the human tendency to shut the ears to God and to listen only to the voices of sin and degradation.

One can easily discern the formidable power of sensuality and lust (Eph. 4:19) to direct the life and to influence the mind of the unbeliever. In Mark 7:21, Christ states that thoughts from within defile a person; people refuse to obey the divine directive (Matt. 18:17; Heb. 2:2). When the heart arrogantly sets itself against God, it has been "blinded" (2 Cor. 4:4) and "led astray" (2 Cor. 11:3) by Satan, so that a person's thoughts oppose all knowledge of God.

Romans 1:18 – 3:20 makes still clearer the impact of sin upon unbelievers. First, Paul demonstrated that knowledge of God has been revealed to the natural man, so that every person is responsible before God. God's attributes are "clearly seen" and "understood" through the created order, and unbelievers are "without excuse" (1:18-20, NIV). However, the mind has been subverted by sin; unbelievers "knew" God but "became futile in their thoughts," so that their "foolish hearts were darkened"[4](1:21).[5] The basic theme is the guilt of man, who has been given a revelation of God yet deliberately rejects it. The remainder of Romans 1 looks to God's judgment upon that rejection. Ernst Käsemann speaks of the "stylistic intensification in the three judgment lists. Portrayal of guilt is increasingly shorter and that of corruption increasingly extensive, culminating in the vice lists of vv. 29-31. . . . The cosmos which will not recognize God's deity in service

4. From *The New King James Version.* Copyright © 1979, 1980, 1982, Thomas Nelson, Inc., Publishers.
5. C. E. B. Cranfield, *A Critical and Exegetical Commentary on the Epistle to the Romans,* International Critical Commentary (Edinburgh: T. & T. Clark, 1975), 1:118, says of the reference to the heart that "it implies no contempt for reason" but is "a sober acknowledgement of the fact that the *kardia* as the inner self of man shares fully in the fallenness of the whole man, that the intellect is not a part of human nature somehow exempted from the general corruption, not something which can be appealed to as an impartial arbiter capable of standing outside the influence of the ego and returning a perfectly objective judgment."

becomes a chaos of unfettered perversion"[6] as God delivers those who reject Him over to their own passions (vv. 24, 26, 28). The sins the unsaved prefer become their masters. So depraved are their minds, they applaud other persons similarly enslaved (1:32).

Sin is personified in Scripture as a malignant force using mind control to try to enslave those made in the image of God. It accomplishes its purpose by deceiving people into wanting its product, much like modern advertisements. James used a metaphor from hunting and fishing to describe the process of temptation, stating that self-centered desires lure and entice men (James 1:14). When a hunter sets a trap, he places something in it the quarry will want. The prey does not sense the presence of the trap until it is sprung. That is the way sin operates: it hides itself under the cover of respectability. Pornography shops, for example, promote themselves by adopting catchy names and mounting clever advertising campaigns geared to snag the young adult. The number of cars at such stores sadly attests that their catch is large.

CONTROLLING THE MIND, EPHESIANS 4:20–24

CONVERSION

The pagan mind-set is the antithesis of the Christward path. As Ephesians 4:20 points out, believers "did not learn Christ in this way." The thoughts of the believer move toward Christ. That is because of the power of conversion to change the mind, as demonstrated in verses 22 and 24: "lay aside the old self . . . put on the new self." The old and new self is a Pauline emphasis, occurring in Romans 6:6, 2 Corinthians 5:17, Colossians 3:10, and elsewhere. In all three passages it is clear that the change takes place at conversion. When an individual is regenerated and justified, the old self dies and is replaced by the new person, made anew in the image of Christ. The imagery means the same today as it did in the first century. When clothes become too soiled they are thrown away and replaced. However, that practice was not as common back then, when garments were so important they were actually handed down from father to son. Therefore, the image Paul used was an extremely strong picture of the

---

6. *Commentary on Romans,* trans. G. W. Bromiley (Grand Rapids: Eerdmans, 1980), p. 44. Cranfield, *Romans,* 1:121, adds the important clarification that God does not "give them over" forever, but rather in a "deliberate act of judgment and mercy . . . smites in order to heal (Isa. 19:22)," that is, forces them to experience the depth of their depravity in order to deal with them.

repugnance of sin. Sin must be laid aside emphatically and with finality.

In Romans 8 Paul presented "the law of the Spirit," which works in antithesis to "the law of sin and of death" and frees one from the enslavement of sin (8:2). In 8:5-7 he described the new mind as sharing the outlook and assumptions of the Spirit, fully committed to the Spirit rather than the flesh. (See Cranfield, *Romans,* 1:386; and J. Goetzman, "Mind," *NIDNTT,* 2:617). Rather than mind control, the Spirit enables believers to control their minds because of His dynamic presence in them (v. 9). The body of sin has died, and the spirit lives a new life of "righteousness" (v. 10).

The idea in Romans 8 fits the imagery of the new clothes in Ephesians 4:24. Because an everyday person received a new set of clothes no more than a couple times in his life, to "put on" new clothes was one of the truly exciting moments in his experience. Paul could have chosen no more apt metaphor to express the joyous moment of conversion.

The involvement of the mind in the conversion process is abundantly clear in the New Testament. It is the heart (associated with the mind) that is the focus of God's redemptive activity. The heart is the conscience God convicts, leading a person to repentance (Acts 2:37; 7:54) and cleansing (Acts 15:9; 16:14). Consequently, the mind is made receptive to divine truths (Rom. 8:27; 1 Cor. 4:5). The new knowledge that results is a gift from God (1 Cor. 2:12; Col. 1:27) and is called divine wisdom, reserved for the elect who are grounded not in speculative, "persuasive words" but in "demonstration of the Spirit and of power" (1 Cor. 2:1-5). This "message of wisdom" is reserved for the "mature" to whom the Spirit reveals the deep, hidden wisdom of the cross (2:6-16, NIV) and who thus have "the mind of Christ" (2:16, NIV), that insight into divine truths or hidden mysteries that is open only to the converted. The key terms are "hidden" and "mystery" as showing the dependence of man upon God for the true wisdom. The opponents drew their wisdom from their own philosophical musings and in the process became "natural" rather than "spiritual" (vv. 13-15).

Robert Jewett, in *Paul's Anthropological Terms* (Leiden: E. J. Brill, 1971, pp. 3-8), argues that Paul equated mind and spirit, saying "we have the Spirit." However, W. D. Stacey's view is probably more accurate. Stacy says that in Pauline thought mind and spirit "are connected but not the same. Possession of the spirit renews man's *nous* [mind] and gives him understanding of the *nous* of Christ. While the two stand together, their functions are quite separate" (*The Pauline View of Man* [London: Macmillan, 1956], p. 203). In this age of high-tech it is more and more common to tap the knowledge of many sources in making decisions. Computers can scan millions of pieces of evidence in milliseconds and draw conclusions that a few years ago would have taken a team of scholars weeks to determine. The "mind of Christ" is similar in that it connotes a new source of information and power for everyday situations. The believer no longer has to think like the natural or carnal person.

However, the fact is that many Christians today do think like the natural or unregenerate person. How do we come to grips with that? The church today needs to recognize the true place of the mind in conversion. The cheap grace or easy-believism that characterizes much of modern evangelistic preaching has no source in the Bible. Mere intellectual assent, as the discussion has shown, will never suffice as an antidote to the depraved mind of secular man. The mind-set or heart of man must be changed. The intellectual side of a person cannot be dichotomized from the volitional, and one can never know Christ as Savior without knowing him as Lord. That does not mean that there are no carnal Christians; rather, it means that a carnal Christian is one who still keeps some areas of his life under the control of self. Christians must fight carnality. As the Puritan John Cotton aptly put it, temptation, like a beast, may scare the Christian off the road, but the real Christian will get back on the road.

POSTCONVERSION

The flesh is the ongoing barrier to the experience of victory by the believer. Although the old self has died, the flesh carries on its activity. In many passages "flesh" is a neutral term depicting only man as a physical entity (1 Cor. 15:39; 2 Cor. 4:11; KJV of Gal. 4:13). However, it is also the primary term for the sinful side of the self. As Jewett observes, it is "not rooted in sensuality but rather in religious rebellion" against God's way (*Paul's Anthropological Terms,* p. 114). A. C. Thiselton defines the flesh as "the outlook oriented towards the self, that which pursues its own ends in self-sufficient independence of God" ("Flesh," *NIDNTT,* 1:680).

We have already seen how life in the Spirit is contrasted to life in the flesh in Romans 8:5–9. The flesh is the link between the preconversion "deeds of the flesh" (immorality, idolatry, anger, and so on, Gal. 5:19–21) and the postconversion sins. Sin uses the flesh to wage war against the spirit and to imprison the believer in prevailing sin (Rom. 7:23). Käsemann, Murray, and others believe Romans 7:7–25 speaks of the unregenerate person, but Cranfield (*Romans,* 1:348) rightly says that the change of tense from past (7–13) to present (14–25) indicates a switch from the preconversion to the postconversion state. The means of obtaining victory over the flesh is dependence upon the power of the Holy Spirit within the believer (Rom. 8). Only in that way can Christians overcome the flesh and become "more than conquerors"[7] (8:37; NIV reading also).

In fact, it is clear from Ephesians 4 that the removal of the old self and the putting on of the new is clearly an application of the conversion metaphor to the ongoing struggle to defeat sin in the life of the believer. Note in v. 22 that the old self "is being corrupted by its deceitful desires" (NIV). The present tense refers to current activity, and the Ephesians are being warned not to allow sin to seduce them into returning to the old deceitful pagan ways described in vv. 17-19. Evil is pictured as a gangrene, slowly rotting and destroying the person. The new self in v. 24 is "created to be like God in true righteousness and holiness" (NIV). Rather than surrendering to the mind-control tactics of sin, the Christian establishes a new, righteous life-style that is recreated in the image of God.

Still, Christians need practical advice as to the means for accomplishing this objective. It is idealistic to pretend that spiritual victory is easily attainable. It is one thing to speak of surrender to the Spirit, quite another thing actually to do so. The fact is that for every hour Christians spend receiving spiritual input via devotions, corporate worship, and fellowship (see the chapters on those topics in this volume), they are likely to receive four or five hours of secular input. The forces arrayed against believers are immense, and Satan moves against them "like a roaring lion" seeking to "devour" (1 Pet. 5:8), or like a harvester wanting to "sift" them "like wheat" (Luke 22:31). Their minds are constantly attacked by a barrage of self-centered models from every quarter, each telling them what they are supposed to be—healthy, wealthy, and wise. In many quarters the "gospel of prosperity" has reversed materialism from a sin to a spiritual goal. (On this, see the excellent article by Gordon Fee, "The 'Gospel' of Prosperity —An Alien Gospel," *Pentecostal Evangel* [24 June 1979], pp. 4-8).

THE BIBLICAL CONCEPT OF RENEWAL

How are Christians to ascertain the will of God in these areas, especially when many Christians have converted worldly concepts into quasi-Christian truth? There is only one answer, and that is found in

---

7. From *The New King James Version.* Copyright © 1979, 1980, 1982, Thomas Nelson, Inc., Publishers.

Ephesians 4:23: the renewal of the mind by the Holy Spirit. Although the verbs in vv. 22 and 24 speak of specific acts of removing, in v. 23 the verb for renewing is a present-tense verb speaking of a continuous act. The renewing of the mind is not accomplished at one time but is a moment-by-moment, step-by-step process. This is spiritual growth in its very essence.

At conversion, the renewal of the mind begins. The mind (or heart) comes under the control of the Holy Spirit and in contrast to the heathen's mind (Eph. 4:17-19) is "renewed" (4:23) in order to "understand what the will of the Lord is" (5:17). These are crucial topics, for in Ephesians Paul focuses on the "heavenlies" as the place of spiritual warfare, where the demonic powers are conquered by the power of Christ (1:3, KJV). That place of warfare includes the mind, and in 4:22-24, as has been seen, the depravity of the heathen mind-set (vv. 17-19) is overcome in a three-stage process: (1) casting off the old self, (2) being renewed in the spirit of one's mind, (3) being clothed with the new self.

Markus Barth, in *Ephesians,* Anchor Bible (Garden City: Doubleday, 1974), 2:542, notes that "clear and rational rethinking, reorientation, and renewal are called for. . . . A renewed mind and a newly dressed body, in short, man's total self is claimed for the service of God." Barth correctly notes that while the language of the passage is grounded in imagery associated with rebirth, the stress is primarily concerned with renewal in daily ethical decisions (pp. 543-45). It is clear that the renewal process is pivotal and provides the means by which the old becomes new.

It is also obvious that personal responsibility is taught here. As in 1 Peter 1:13, believers are to "prepare" (NIV) their minds; and as in 2 Corinthians 10:4-5, they are to control, or "take captive" (NIV), every thought in obedience to Christ (note the context of warfare). In Ephesians 5:17, the one who wisely (v. 15) uses his time (v. 16) will seek to "understand" God's will, a concept parallel to 1 Corinthians 2:16. The believer's mind is seen as a battleground between opposing forces, and spiritual victory is seen as being dependent upon the rigid control of every thought that results from the renewal of the mind by Christ. As Markus Barth states, "There still has to take place an increase in comprehension of the Lord's will (Eph. 5:10, 17), a radical severance from evil deeds and words (Eph. 5:3-7, 11-12), and a wise exploitation of the opportunities of the present time" (*Ephesians,* 2:603).

Barth notes also that the recognition of God's will is the climax of Ephesians 5:1-20, and he delineates four aspects of obedience: (1) it involves intellectual activity, (vv. 10, 17), (2) it contains a social dimension, i.e., an involvement in community, by which the victory over the powers of darkness is experienced, (3) it must be expressed in the believer's total conduct, not just in individual good deeds, (4) it is a joyous, emotional celebration of victory in the community life (*Ephesians,* 2:604). When believers conduct their lives as "children of light" (v. 8), they will be enabled to discern that which pleases God from that which is "unfruitful" (vv. 10-11).

The idea parallels Romans 12:1-2, a passage critical in the development of Romans, because it marks the transition from the doctrinal to the practical. After painting a vast panorama of salvation from sin in chapters 1-11, Paul bridged the gap to the ethical responsibilities that ensue. The presentation (cp. 6:13, 16, 19) of one's total self to God as a "sacrifice" is the basis of the ethical stance and is characterized by three qualities: it is "living" in the sense of expressing the new life in Christ; it is "holy" in the sense of experiencing the set-apartness that characterizes the sanctified; it is "acceptable to God" in the sense that it pleases Him.[8] Finally, the presentation of oneself must be done in the spirit of rational worship,[9] that involvement of the whole being in true worship of God.

The mind is a critical part of the entire process, as demonstrated in Romans 12:2. At the outset, there is no distinction between conform (as if it refers to outward appearance) and transform (as if it means inward essence); both refer to the powers brought to bear upon a person so as to produce change. The message in v. 2 clarifies v. 1, telling the reader how that sacrificial presentation is to be accomplished. He must avoid the influence of "this world," which continually pressures him to conform to its mold, to become culture-bound to its fleeting fashions. Rather, the believer must allow God to transform his spiritual faculties by "the renewing of [his] mind." Clearly, the process is not accomplished by active learning but rather by passive surrender to the presence of the Spirit (cf. Romans 8). Yet it distinctly involves one's mind-set, which must undergo the continuous renewing process already noted in Ephesians 4:17-24. As Furnish says, the similar vocabulary in Romans 1 and 12 makes it obvious that in Romans 12 Paul

---

8. See Cranfield, *Romans,* 2:600-611. Käsemann, *Romans,* p. 327, challenges Cranfield's ethical interpretation of "holy" and prefers an eschatological approach, i.e., "open to God's present time and manifesting this." However, the context favors an ethical stance.

9. Although C. K. Barrett, *A Commentary on the Epistle to the Romans* (London: Adam and Charles Black, 1971), p. 231, and others argue for the translation "spiritual worship," I agree with Cranfield (pp. 602-5) that "rational" in the sense of a true understanding of divine principles is superior. (Note how this follows both the usage of "body" and "acceptable" here.)

is speaking of the antithesis of the "depraved mind" (NIV) of the natural man; thus "Romans 12:1-2 is but the restatement . . . of the theme which had already been emphasized in 1:16–17" (Victor Paul Furnish, *Theology and Ethics in Paul* [Nashville: Abingdon, 1968], p. 103).

The purpose of this renewal is to enable the believer to test or discern the will of God. The idea thus being put forth resembles the teachings of Ephesians 5:10, 17. Before the mind can attain discernment of the will of God, Paul says, it must undergo the Spirit's process of restoration and renewal. Only then can a person discern properly God's will and directives. Robin Scroggs calls this greater capacity of perception "depth knowledge" (*Paul for a New Day* [Philadelphia: Fortress, 1977], p. 59). It develops when one has conquered self-centered thinking and has allowed God so to transform the ability to perceive reality that one's mind is literally opened to God's mind.

As a result, God's will is proved to be "good and acceptable and perfect" (12:2). Most commentators take at least the second and perhaps all three adjectives to refer to the believer's standing before God rather than to the impact of God's will upon his life. In this light the statement is often seen as being parallel to the characteristics at the end of 12:1. I have never been convinced by that argument. The key in the discussion is the relationship between the terms. Most argue on the basis of verse 1 and the use of *euareston* in the New Testament (all but one, Titus 2:9, refer to God) that "acceptable" means "to God" rather than "to me." G. Delling argues similarly for *teleion;* it refers to knowledge of the "perfect" or "entire" will of God.[10] Yet the differences over the interpretation of the term do not obviate the view that God's will is perfect "for me." Romans 12:1 dealt with the believer's presentation to God, and therefore the adjectives in the verse clarified the way the believer's sacrifices are related to God. In 12:2, however, the context concerns the believer's discernment of God's will with respect to the believer's own situation. Such an interpretation fits the thrust of *dokimazo.* The person who tests a thing does so with respect to his own decision. Therefore, it seems preferable to think that believers test or prove that God's will is "good" and "acceptable" and "perfect" for them. The verses build upon rather than restate their respective messages. In verse 1, a Christian's sacrificial presentation of his total self to God is living, holy, and acceptable in His sight. In verse 2 the focus shifts, for as a result of their spiritual renewal, Christians are enabled to

10. *"Teleios," Theological Dictionary of the New Testament* (hereafter, *TDNT*), 8:76. See also Cranfield, *Romans,* pp. 610–11.

discern the value of God's will for their lives. In verse 1 believers give themselves to God; in verse 2 He returns that gift to them, as His will becomes operative in their lives.

When the renewal process does its proper work, the seemingly impossible ethical demands of the New Testament (for example, those in the Sermon on the Mount) or of Jesus' radical teaching on discipleship become more understandable. Most of the expectations are predicated upon the Spirit's presence and work in one's life. For instance, hearing means doing (Luke 11:28; Rom. 2:13; and especially James 1:22-27), and knowing is equated with obeying (2 Cor. 10:5-6). Christians must appropriate and use God's wisdom (Eph. 5:5; James 1:3; 5:20) in every area of life, that is, they must recognize what is right in any situation and do it (James 4:17). In John, hearing becomes mutual knowledge and is equated with fellowship with both Father and Son (10:14-15).

The result of love's abounding in the sphere of knowledge and insight is the ability to test or discern the superior things in life (Phil. 1:9-10), a concept that parallels Romans 12:2 and Ephesians 5:17. As already stated, testing is the ability to investigate and determine the worthiness of the important things in life (Rom. 2:18; 12:2; Eph. 5:10; Phil. 1:10). All things must be tested in this way (1 Thess. 5:21), especially one's self (1 Cor. 11:28; 2 Cor. 13:5; Gal. 6:4). God often tests believers (1 Thess. 2:4; Rom. 14:10), frequently through trials (James 1:3; 1 Pet. 1:7), in order to prove them to be genuine. The one who endures the test is approved by knowing God's will (Rom. 12:2; Eph. 5:17) and doing that which pleases Him (Rom. 12:1; Phil. 1:10; Eph. 5:10). The Christian who fails the test is "disqualified" (1 Cor. 9:27).

Discipline and community are two further ingredients necessary to ensure proper spiritual growth. Because God reckons us righteous (Rom. 4:3-5, 22-24; 2 Cor. 5:18-19; James 2:23), we are to reckon our thoughts "captive" for Him (2 Cor. 10:4-7), resulting in actions that follow disciplined evaluation (Rom. 14:14; Phil. 4:8-9). As H. W. Heidland demonstrates, the progress of the concept is as follows: previously our "rational judgments" were controlled by enemy forces and thus were hostile to God, that is, "the thoughts of a reason which in its self-vaunting shuts itself off from God" (*"logizomai," TNDT,* 4:287). The only solution lay in the power of God as manifested at the cross; God's power thus manifested created the downfall of human reason and caused "the collapse of heaven-storming reason before the revelation of this reason" (Heidland, p. 21). As a result, the believer is made the victor and can now take "every thought captive to the obedience of Christ" (2 Cor. 10:5). The Spirit renews and reorients one's thinking capacity so that it can properly judge spiritual options

(Rom. 6:11; 8:18; 14:14; Phil. 3:13) and live a life of spiritual victory. Yet the personal responsibility is not thereby minimized. There is a distinct contrast between "the enemies of the cross" whose "minds are on earthly things" (Phil. 3:18-19, probably a church-related group) and true believers, who set their minds "on the things above, not on the things that are on earth" (Col. 3:2).

The same mental discipline is to be reflected in the community life of the church. Rather than a disunity centering upon selfish ambition leading to a party-spirit, i.e., the splitting up of the church into warring factions (2 Cor. 12:20; Phil. 1:17; 2:3; James 3:14, 16), believers are urged to be united in thought or attitude (Phil. 2:2, where the concept is repeated twice; cf. 3:15; 4:2; Rom. 12:16; 15:5; 2 Cor. 13:11; negatively in Gal. 5:10). The passages just cited show the importance of that truth for the early church: spiritual growth is corporate as well as individual. Most of the passages discussed thus far are distinctly oriented to the individual as a member of the body of Christ. That is illustrated by the motif "in Christ," which at one time was interpreted in terms of a mystical union or communion with Christ (e.g., Deissman), but increasingly has come to be identified with the unity of believers in Christ. (See Herman Ridderbos, *Paul: An Outline of His Theology,* trans. John Richard DeWitt [Grand Rapids: Eerdmans, 1977], pp. 58-64; Murray Harris, "Prepositions and Theology in the Greek New Testament," NIDNTT, 3:1192, Barth, *Ephesians,* 1:69-71.) The individual, though still primarily identified with Christ, is seen now as existing in community.

The mental or attitudinal aspect of this unity is crucial: one who is "in Christ" must "regard" others as "more important than himself" (Phil. 2:3); and the model for that is Christ (Phil. 2:5), so that the believer's mind becomes identified with His.[11] As Paul stated in Romans 12:16, the keynote of this corporate attitude is humility as the antithesis to a haughty mind-set (cf. Rom 11:20; 1 Tim. 6:17) that exalts self and puts it upon the throne of one's life. Only thereby can the community properly glorify God (Rom. 15:5-6).

The topic is a critical one for a church today. Christians sometimes separate from one another more over personality clashes than over

---

11. The interpretation of 2:5 in light of the hymn which follows is exceedingly complex. See Ralph P. Martin, *Philippians,* New Century Bible (Greenwood, S.C.: Attic, 1976), p. 91, for a good survey of the options. I believe the "paradigmatic" approach, which looks to Christ as the model for us, is superior to Martin's preference, the "drama of salvation" view, which denigrates the connection between Jesus' exaltation and ours in the context. Rather, both his humility (centering on his servanthood) and his exaltation (which he left up to God) are proper patterns for us.

doctrinal matters. Personal disputes cripple true spiritual renewal. Until believers learn to empathize with other people before they react against them, God's work will be hindered. That is true at the deepest level of Christian interrelationships, the family (1 Pet. 3:7, where prayers can "be hindered"), and it is equally true of the body of Christ as a whole (note especially the connection between all believers in Eph. 5:21 and the husband-wife relationship as a microcosm of the church in 5:22-32).

CONCLUSION

Spiritual renewal is first of all a reshaping of the believer's mental outlook, a restoration of his life's pattern to its proper place with God. It opens his total being to new vistas of understanding and new sources of spiritual power, so that he may go on the offensive and capture his thoughts for the glory of Christ. That is the essence of discipleship. Failure occurs when his thoughts are controlled by human desires and therefore by Satan (e.g., Peter in Mark 8:33 and parallels), but victory ensues whenever the believer makes a radical commitment to Christ and refuses to look back to the old patterns of living (Luke 9:57-62). As such, the Christian must deny self, which means he must "take up his cross daily," that is, consider his old ways and relationships dead (Luke 9:23; 14:27). Such denial can be accomplished only when he counts the cost (Luke 14:28-31) and surrenders himself to God (Luke 14:32).

Spiritual renewal also means commitment to other Christians. But some believers have become so caught up in looking out for themselves that they have lost the ability to relate to others. Sometimes people hesitate to open up to others because they have a low self-image and fear that others will reject them if they know what they are really like, or they fear that others might use their weaknesses against them. Yet openness to others plays a major role in spiritual renewal. In the midst of the pressures brought to bear upon the Jewish Christians in the first century, the writer of the epistle to the Hebrews stressed again and again that victory was dependent upon the corporate unity of the body. First, Christians must deal with the problem of sin: "Encourage one another day after day . . . lest any one of you be hardened by the deceitfulness of sin" (Heb. 3:13). The "rest" theology of chapters 3-4 is corporate (e.g., 4:9, "for the people of God") as well as individual; exhortation is a key responsibility of fellowship between all believers. Second, Christians must deal with encouragement: "Not forsaking our own assembling together . . . but encouraging one another" (10:25). It is interesting that the same term is used for both "exhort" and "encourage," two words for the same act.

Encouragement is especially needed with respect to weak Christians, as seen in Hebrews 12-13. After the important discussion of God's disciplining process (12:4-11), the writer concludes ("therefore") that the church must become a restoration center (note the parallel with the Spirit's activity in Rom. 12:2) for the weaker members by making "straight paths" for the weak so that they may be "healed" rather than being "put out of joint" (Heb. 12:12-13). In so doing the church must avoid the "root of bitterness" (cf. Deut. 29:18) that can develop and defile the community (12:15). Bitterness can be avoided through "love" and "hospitality" (13:1-2), which themselves spring from a spirit of contentment caused by the confidence that God is continually on one's side (13:5-6).

When all of the material above is put together, there are apparently seven steps in the process of renewing the mind according to the biblical pattern: (1) In the experience of conversion God puts to death the old self and mind-set, rejuvenating the spirit in newness of life. (2) That action makes it possible for Christians to prepare their minds (1 Pet. 1:13) to accept the ongoing discipline and control of the Holy Spirit (John 16:13). (3) Next, every thought must be taken captive in obedience to Christ (part of the cosmic war, 2 Cor. 10:4-5). (4) Believers must allow the Spirit continually to renew their mind-set (Rom. 12:2; Eph. 4:23). (5) Because they have a new mental outlook, believers will begin to discern and understand the will of God (Rom. 12:2; Eph. 5:17). (6) The control of the mind that results will cause Christians to become a living demonstration to all that God's will indeed is "good and acceptable and perfect" (Rom. 12:2). (7) The resulting harmony will be corporate: the church will be "united in spirit, intent on one purpose" (Phil. 2:2), so that as a body-fellowship it can experience prayer power (Phil. 4:6-7; thus "the peace of God") and a controlled mind (Phil. 4:8-9; thus "the God of peace"). Each of the seven steps will be one of movement from mind-control to a Spirit-endowed control of the mind, the essence of spiritual growth.

In short, renewing the mind is an important antidote to the strange illness that has overtaken the church in our generation. Yet there is justification for having optimism for the future. A new era is approaching. When I speak to churches and para-church groups, I detect a hunger for genuine Bible teaching and a growing awareness of the difference between deep and shallow teaching. There seems to be a true desire for spiritual renewal and a restoration of the foci of teaching and fellowship at the core of the church. There are exciting days ahead.

Part 3

The Daily Challenge in Renewing Our Minds

5 The Christian's Resources in the Local Church

David Larsen

It would be a serious mistake to consider the renewing of the Christian's mind as exclusively an individual matter. John Wesley was right in his insistence that the Bible knows nothing of solitary religion. To come into a new relationship with God through Christ means we have come into a new relationship with the household of faith. We become part of the believing community, the new people of God. The church is the sign of the new age.

Every description of the church used in the New Testament emphasizes the interrelatedness of believers in Christ. As the Body of Christ, the church consists of many diverse parts working together in extraordinary harmony and efficiency. As the bride of Christ, the church is to experience and express deep caring and mutual affection. As the building of God, the church is to expand and enlarge as people come to Christ and believers are built up. As branches in the true vine, believers in the church are to bear fruit to the glory of God. Believers in Christ are functioning parts of a supernatural spiritual organism, the church. This reality has significant implications for the renewing of the mind.

Too often our experience of genuine spiritual community is deficient. Many believers feel, like Kipling's famous cat, "out on his wild lone."

David Larsen (B.A., Stanford University; M.Div., Fuller Theological Seminary) is associate professor of practical theology at Trinity Evangelical Divinity School. He has had a fruitful pastoral ministry in North Dakota, Minnesota, California, and Illinois.

That may be due in part to an exaggerated individualism in Western culture. With little sensitivity to our rich heritage, and torn loose from any real awareness of continuity, we are proud of being self-made persons. "I am a self-made man," one man boasted. Were that true, it would relieve the Almighty of considerable responsibility, and it would also underscore the disaster of unskilled labor. In point of fact, we are debtors. Tennyson reminds us that we are part of all we have met. The apostle Paul insisted: "We brought nothing into the world, and we can take nothing out of it" (1 Tim. 6:7, NIV). We are all the beneficiaries of God's grace through the many who have gone before us and bequeathed us innumerable legacies physically, intellectually, emotionally, aesthetically, and above all, spiritually.

Any believer who pretends to be the Lone Ranger is not facing reality. Believers need each other in the spiritual battle in which they engage. Harvie Conn (*Evangelism, Doing Justice and Preaching Grace* [Grand Rapids: Zondervan, 1982], p. 18) has recently written of the danger and myth of "privatization" among evangelicals:

> Recent research underlines the growing power of the privatization myth of the evangelical. Built out of the American model of the rugged individual, it reduces sin's social dimensions into individual sins, and compartmentalizes our lives into dichotomies—sacred and secular, private and public sectors, stay-in and stay-out zones. It is reflected in the Gallup poll that found that 76 percent of those who go to church (and 86 percent of the unchurched) agree that "an individual should arrive at his or her own religious beliefs independent of any churches or synagogues."

On the contrary, Scripture insists that we are bound together in the bundle of life and that our interdependency as believers bears significantly on the renewing of our minds.

Sin has been a total disaster for the whole person. With respect to the mind, the apostle Paul makes clear that "the mind of sinful man is death, but the mind controlled by the Spirit is life and peace, because the sinful mind is hostile toward God" (Rom. 8:6, NIV; see also Rom. 1:28; 2 Cor. 3:14; 4:4; 2 Tim. 3:8).

In salvation God renews the whole person after the image of God. When controlled by the Holy Spirit the mind is made new in its attitudes (Eph. 4:23). Whereas Satan seeks to corrupt, defile, confuse, unsettle and discourage the mind, the Holy Spirit seeks to renew, guide, enlighten, and quicken the mind in the thoughts and counsels of God (Rom. 12:2; 2 Cor. 10:4-5).

The renewed mind is characterized by steady attention to God and

His truth; a deepening understanding of God and His truth; obedient submission to God and His truth; and increasing affection for God and His truth (Luke 10:25-28). In the achievement of those ends, our corporate experience in the Body of Christ makes a significant contribution. But how is it that authentic experience of Christian community fosters and facilitates the achievement of these objectives?

CHRISTIAN FRIENDSHIP AND FELLOWSHIP ENRICH THE MIND

The new birth is the initial step in the process of renewal described in the New Testament. (See B. B. Warfield, "On the Biblical Notion of 'Renewal,'" in *Biblical and Theological Studies* [Nutley, N.J.: Presb. & Ref., 1968], pp. 351-74.) Faith, however, though personal is not private. The Christian becomes part of the family of God (1 John 3:1). No believer is an only child. We have brothers and sisters in the family. The very diversity within that glorious unity greatly enriches life.

In the brokenness and fragmentation of modern life, in the despairing sense of alienation and estrangement, many people have a great longing for belonging. That perhaps explains why Americans are such great joiners. The atomization of society has given rise to a craving for community. People feel they are only statistics. It is little wonder that collectivisms of various kinds have appeal to many. We see the television soaps as fantasy communities and therefore as highly appealing.

The church of Jesus Christ offers something unique. There may be facsimiles of it, but there is no adequate equivalent. That is what is termed *fellowship* in the New Testament. The word means, literally, "having something in common with someone else." In Scripture the word conveys the idea of inward union. The earliest usage of the term is in Acts 2:42: "They were continually devoting themselves to the apostles' teaching and to fellowship." It was a favorite term for the marriage contract in the times of Augustus.

What may pass for fellowship in the church oftentimes is a kind of cheek by jowl, hip by haunch proximity, stoked by greasy hot dogs and creamy cole slaw. It can be artificial, shallow, trite, and tending strongly to gossip. Yet many echo Emerson's plaint, "I am weary of the surfaces." New Testament fellowship is at a deep level of communication, of sharing, of giving and receiving, of participation. That fellowship is exemplified in the breaking of bread in the Lord's Supper. The single loaf and the cup express this "unity of the Spirit in the bond of peace" (Eph. 4:3). Proof of the fellowship is generosity, fellow-feeling, indeed the giving of tangible contributions and support.

The fellowship of kindred minds
Is like to that above.

Such bonds of mutuality and reciprocity are an incredibly rich resource for the spiritual pilgrim. This is "the communion of saints," that deep awareness of a truly spiritual and supportive togetherness in Jesus Christ. In recent years we have witnessed the rapid spread of the small-group movement in the churches. Such a proliferation speaks to a felt need. It is not enough to plunk oneself down in a church service and hear choirs and preaching. Being part of the body of Christ necessitates ministering one to another, breaking down the barriers and obstacles to communication and openness.

When Paul was on his way to Rome and endured many trials in the course of his journey (we read in Acts 28:15, NIV), he met Christian brothers who had come out to welcome him: "At the sight of these men, Paul thanked God and was encouraged." Bunyan pictures Christian and Faithful making their way through the Valley of the Shadow and notes how "they went very lovingly on together, and had sweet discourse of all things that had happened to them in their Pilgrimage." Their companionship was a beautiful providence and aided them immeasurably to traverse the treacherous and difficult terrain. It is a fact that geese flying in formation fly seventy percent faster than a single goose flies.[1]

Several recent studies have dealt helpfully with the "one another" passages of the New Testament. Those Scriptures stake out the way toward the realization of the kind of community that helps us in the renewing of our minds. We are to be "devoted to one another" (Rom. 12:10, NIV). We are to "honor one another" (Rom. 12:10, NIV). We are to be "of the same mind with one another" (Rom. 15:5). We are to "accept one another" (Rom. 15:7). We are to "instruct one another" (Rom. 15:14, NIV). We are to "greet one another" (Rom. 16:16, NIV).

SUPPORT STRUCTURES

Jesus told His own, "I have called you friends" (John 15:15, NIV). Friendship is a key factor in the coming of people to Christ. Seven hundred twenty people who had received the gospel with varying responses were asked to classify the person who had told them about

1. Browne Barr, *High-Flying Geese: Unexpected Reflections on the Church and Its Ministry* (New York: Seabury, 1982), p. 1.

Christ into one of three categories: friend, salesman, or teacher. Of those who saw the church member as a friend, 94 percent had made a decision for Christ and were involved and active in a church. Of those who saw the church member as a salesman, 71 percent made a decision for Christ and then dropped out of church life. Of those who saw the church member as a teacher, 84 percent decided not to receive Christ as their Savior. We need Christian friends. My wife is my best friend. We all need friends who can sit down with us and look us squarely in the eye and lovingly communicate to us where we are moving from the track of good judgment and balance. "Perfume and incense bring joy to the heart, and the pleasantness of one's friend springs from his earnest counsel" (Prov. 27:9, NIV). "As iron sharpens iron, so one man sharpens another" (Prov. 27:17, NIV). Honesty, transparency, and unconditional love are the foundations of true friendship. When I visited the Florida home of Thomas Edison, I was fascinated by a path in his garden called "The Walk of Friendship." It was so named because each stone was given by a different close acquaintance of the inventor. That path is symbolic because we all walk on stones of helpfulness provided by our friends.

As early as the 1830s, Alexis de Tocqueville wrote about the loneliness of Americans, describing the citizens of this country as "locked in the solitude of their own hearts." That has not substantially changed. People no longer have communities to which they are irrevocably tied. One sociologist explains, "Communities are brittle, fragile, with a tremendous turnover." In *Megatrends* John Naisbitt makes a compelling case for the need of high-touch in our increasingly high-tech age. Working has traditionally offered opportunities for companionship and society. But a sense of being part of something is rarely offered in the complexity of corporate life. An increasing number of people now work alone and suffer because of it. F. W. Robertson's great sermon "The Loneliness of Christ" contrasts two kinds of solitude: isolation in space, that is, separation caused by distance, and the more devastating, isolation of spirit, or the loneliness of the soul. The latter is the nagging and remorseless anguish experienced by many. What an opportunity for the church of Jesus Christ.

Every local congregation needs a network of support groups. Those are variously called growth groups, or 2:7 groups, or some such. The need for such groups is true even in large congregations where the church serves as a refuge for those shy or reticent persons who wish to fade into the background of a more anonymous existence.

WE NEED TO STUDY THE BIBLE TOGETHER

Everyone should be part of a small group Bible study discussion. Effective leaders of those groups are concerned to create a relaxed environment in which people feel free to express their own ideas. Sharing insights from heart to heart is one of the most satisfying of all human experiences. We learn from one another. I have never met a human being from whom I could not learn something. People are interesting. It is heartening to see the great growth of interest in Bible study throughout our country. People are digging into the Scriptures for themselves, and many who want to tackle solid material and experience the stimulation of dialogue are joining Bible book discussion groups.

WE NEED TO PRAY TOGETHER

Every believer should be part of a regular prayer tryst. The apostle Paul in his exquisite prayer for the Ephesian believers in Ephesians 3:14–21 prays: "And I pray that you, being rooted and established in love, may have power, together with all the saints, to grasp how wide and long and high and deep is the love of Christ, and to know this love that surpasses knowledge—that you may be filled to the measure of all the fullness of God" (NIV). We are conscious that each of us perceives the oceanic and infinite love of Christ from a slightly different perspective. It is when we are "together with all the saints" that we begin to comprehend in a more full and complete sense the panoramic and sweeping horizons of the divine love. It is ominous indeed that the prayer meeting is passing from the American evangelical scene. The following considerations should be weighed in thinking of this vital facet of spiritual experience:

1. A meaty but more brief Bible study should be part of the prayer meeting.
2. If at all possible the larger group should be broken into smaller units for prayer.
3. Duplicated prayer bulletins should be distributed in the interests of specificity and accuracy in the concerns of prayer.
4. Public prayer should not be primarily a recital of physical maladies or an opportunity to make announcements.
5. Sometimes sentence prayers—conversational prayer—should be encouraged by the leaders.
6. Special early morning men's prayer meetings, or prayer breakfasts,

or downtown prayer meetings at noon, or women's prayer meetings, or youth missionary volunteer's prayer meetings should be encouraged.

7. Periodic twelve- or twenty-four-hour prayer vigils are a meaningful experience for many.

8. Observance of the Annual Day of Prayer in March or the Universal Week of Prayer during the first full week of January should be rejuvenated by fresh and creative variations such as an annual school of prayer, or by joint prayer meetings with other evangelical churches in the area.

9. Clear biblical teaching should be shared on the important relationship between fasting and prayer.[2]

The life of personal and family prayer can easily stagnate if there is not a regular experience of united and corporate prayer. Corporate prayer is a critical area in the renewing of the mind in modern America. The book of Acts presents a compelling portrait of the early believers: "They were all together" (Acts 2:1). The efficacy and power of united, prevailing prayer are brought home again and again (cf. Acts 4, 12, and so on).

WE NEED TO MINISTER TO EACH OTHER

The New Testament portrays the church of Jesus Christ as a fellowship of the concerned. The relational ties are to be such that "if one part suffers, every part suffers with it; if one part is honored, every part rejoices with it" (1 Cor. 12:26, NIV). When we falter and are hard-pressed, sometimes the church is the last place we wish it known. We Christians can be very hard on one another. We can be extremely competitive and can operate on the basis of jealousy and envy. We can become masters of facade and pretense. We can make keeping up appearances a paramount value.

The members of some religious cults and of some ethnic groups seem to be more dedicated to each other than are we whose love for each is to make us conspicuous in the world (John 13:35). Are Christians the kind who will shoot their wounded? It should be possible, without any compromise of Scriptural conviction and moral standards, for believers to create through the enablement of the Holy Spirit an accepting atmosphere in which the bruised and beaten can find refuge and understanding. Jesus Himself exemplified the gentleness and

2. On this last, see Richard J. Foster, "Fasting," in *The Celebration of Discipline* (New York: Harper & Row, 1978), 1:41–53.

tenderness which gave Him a powerful ministry to the disinherited, the disenfranchaised, and the downcast of earth. Contemporary evangelicals must beware of the snare of spiritual sophistication and material affluence that isolates them from and makes them inaccessible to people who are in severe difficulty.

The mandate of Scripture is clear as to our responsibility to one another. In the battles for the mind and spirit, we have an obligation of watchcare and concern for one another. Paul wrote to the Galatians: "Brothers, if a man is trapped in some sin, you who are spiritual should restore him gently" (Gal. 6:1, NIV). The apostle used a medical term describing the resetting of a fractured limb. Such spiritual ministration calls for an exacting qualification: "you who are spiritual." This is not a time for proud and self-seeking motives. It would be possible to take advantage of a fallen or failing brother. It would be possible to look down on him or to patronize, manipulate, or exploit him in a time of crisis and tailspin. But we ought to minister to him gently and responsibly. All of this is to be within a clear frame-of-reference: "Carry each other's burdens, and in this way you will fulfill the law of Christ" (Gal. 6:2, NIV). Putting the matter in practical terms, the stakes are so high and the struggle so intense, we are obliged to go to the aid of our brothers and sisters when they are in trouble. We must be more confrontive as individuals and as spiritual leaders. Early intervention may be advisable to avert later disasters. Such intervention must have been preceded by the developing of significant ties and relationships that can bear the freight of serious spiritual discussion. We must communicate genuine love and concern. Studies show there is less suicide where there is a closely-knit supportive network.

L. H. Bugbee made a similar point in his description of the seige of Constantinople by the Turks in the fifteenth century. When "the Christian garrison was hard-pressed, they sent for the priests and the monks, that they might go up and down the lines encouraging the troops and imparting spiritual reassurance. But the churchmen sent back word that it would . . . interrupt their period of formal worship and devotion; therefore they begged to be excused" (*Daily Bread,* Radio Bible class, 30 June 1983). When we see a believer who needs help, or if a believer appeals to us for help, our temptation is to pass "by on the other side" (Luke 10:31, NIV). We can excuse ourselves because we lack skill, time, or expertise. There is risk in going to the aid of a troubled comrade. Who knows what kind of an imposition might result? Isn't it wiser just not to become involved? We must take risks. The good Samaritan did. It cost him time and means to tend to the man beset by thieves and left to die. Believers caught in a tragic marital situation or victimized by financial or vocational problems can find loneliness and desolation compounding the difficulties. Believers who know such persons ought to help them, in a spirit of love and compassion.

Priscilla and Aquila heard the brilliant Christian orator, Apollos, "a learned man, with a thorough knowledge of the Scriptures" (Acts 18:24, NIV). They were artisans and craftsmen, but they did not capitulate to a sense of inferiority or inadequacy. They were not intimidated. They saw the need of Apollos and took a bold initiative. "They invited him to their home and explained to him the way of God more adequately" (Acts 18:26, NIV). We need to see the possibilities of the practical ministry of hospitality. Let us break out of the rut of our little clique and invite others to come in. A modest but attractively served meal speaks to the foreign student, the lonely single, the college student or serviceman or servicewoman far from home. The lines of friendship are deeply satisfying. Through them we learn about and gain insight in communicating with people outside of our comfortable and congenial set. We have opportunity to minister.

The climate and atmosphere in the local congregation will determine whether the saints are seen as a museum for the perfect or a hospital for those who are being made well. Our tone in proclamation can create a mood and a setting that are threatening to those who hesitate or who struggle with uncertainty and doubt. Must every issue be resolved immediately and instantaneously? Do we have the maturity to sustain the tension of some ambiguity, or are we so insecure as to require everyone to dot each *i* and cross each *t* in precisely and exactly the same way? David Shipler has recently pointed out that the entire Russian educational system is focused on building such certainty into the minds of the people that "by the time many Russians reach their teens they have already developed a virulent allergy to ambiguity" (*Russia: Broken Idols, Solemn Dreams* [Times, 1983]). We do not in fact have all the answers. Where Scripture does not speak certainly, we cannot speak certainly. It is the cultic mind that sees all issues with the same certainty and force as the virgin birth of Christ. We must allow freedom of opinion where Scripture does not bind us.

The church can become so engaged in pressing for cultural conformity that its efforts are counterproductive. The minutia of dress, speech, and life-style can loom into major issues that divide the body of Christ. Must I always be right? Can I listen to views of truth differing from my own? Do I panic when someone articulates a different perception? Paul's philosophy of becoming "all things to all men" that he "might by all means save some" (1 Cor. 9:22, KJV) has been twisted and turned pathetically and wrongly to be sure. Yet the apostle went to great lengths to keep open the channel of communication to Jewish elements in Jerusalem. Perhaps he went too far in taking the vow and shaving his head. God must be his judge. Yet is is clear that he desperately desired not to hinder and inhibit the gospel message by side issues and secondary differences.

In view, then, of the war for the mind and in view of revealed truth, it is imperative that spiritually-minded and sensitive believers ever be looking for brothers and sisters in need — and then, in the context of the church, and in the context of exercising effective interpersonal relationships, they should address those needs.

WE NEED TO ENCOURAGE EACH OTHER

The modern mind is clearly "sick unto death." All the media incessantly bombard us with appeals to the grossest of our instincts. H. G. Wells spoke at the end of his life of his "mind at the end of its tether." Everything seems to conspire to pull us down. Many people are depressed and pessimistic. Christians should stand out as those who have hope and expectancy for the future.

We need to have concern for encouraging people whom we meet. I am not pleading for superficiality or artificiality, but I am saying that we will do well to ponder the significance of the seemingly insignificant. After all, great doors swing on small hinges. There is a positive, kindly, thoughtful word or inquiry that can mean much to a human being who is having tough sledding. A solicitous phone call or a letter of appreciation at that time would mean much more than a spray of flowers for a funeral.

Jesus always impresses us with His fairness and His unfailing courtesy. He was thoughtful and appreciative. He sent His disciples to obtain the donkey for the Palm Sunday event, and He included the gracious and thoughtful words: "The Lord has need of it and will send it back here immediately" (E. F. Harrison, *A Short Life of Christ* [Grand Rapids: Eerdmans, 1968], p. 258).

Am I an encourager? Are you an encourager? A singing and hearty Danish street car conductor brightened a dark, cold wintry morning for his passengers each day. Not all are extroverts as he was, but he made an indelible impression on my mind. It is so easy to be inward, withdrawn, immersed so totally in our own affairs that we do not pick up the cues and signals from the distressed and distraught. A little extra effort can make a big difference to a soul struggling to stay out of the depth of despair. A word spoken from Jesus. A quiet breath of prayer. A kindly pat on the back. A warm smile. They can mean more than we imagine. Such concern should be normal in the Christian community, both toward those within and toward those without. Let us scatter flowers by the wayside as we journey on toward "the city with foundations, whose architect and builder is God" (Heb. 11:10, NIV).

THE WORSHIP OF GOD "IN SPIRIT AND IN TRUTH" EXPANDS THE MIND

The true worship of the living God must be seen as crucial in the renewing of the mind. This worship is intensely personal and inevitably corporate. Karl Barth has said that Christian worship is "the most momentous, the most urgent, the most glorious action that can take place in human life." Worship is the practice of the heart's devotion to God. That is the personal and individual experience. But worship is the presence of the living God among His people. That is the corporate aspect. God seeks true worshipers (John 4:23).

Daniel the prophet prayed with his window opened toward Jerusalem. Worship is the opening of our souls to God. We do not want to live in a house without windows. Every aspect of our lives needs this opening of our beings to the reality of the power and presence of the Almighty God. Paul Scherer asserts, "Worship is that time when we bring the gods we have made before the God who has made us." We all must wrestle with the idols of the mind. Whitehead maintained that idolatry is contentment with the prevalent gods. We need the regular and consistent turning of the thoughts and intents of the mind and heart over to God in worship. Our worship must focus on the greatness of God more than upon our needs. Worship is admiration, fascination, adoration, and celebration (See A. W. Tozer, *Worship: The Missing Jewel of the Evangelical Church* [Christian Publication, n.d.]).

In many of our evangelical traditions, worship has been thin and weak. We have reveled in a free liturgy. In our concern that we not have too much form we have become careless of any form. No form, after all, is bad form. Many evangelical seminaries require no course in worship and liturgics. Some of the movement in evangelical circles toward high church worship is a reaction against the slipshod and careless approach in evangelical worship. Tozer was right when he spoke of worship as "the missing jewel of the evangelical church." There is heartening evidence that that jewel may be in process of recovery. Such a recovery would be most salutary for evangelicals at this juncture and would be highly relevant for the church in the pitched battle it must fight for the mind.

On one occasion Robert Louis Stevenson returned from church and reported: "I've been to church and I am not depressed." So many do not look forward to the services of worship. For them the statement in the bulletin "Morning Worship Service at 11:00 A.M." is not accurate but highly presumptuous. Too many are bored by the sameness, the lameness, the tameness of the service. We are being done in by a kind of total predictability. Yet others would turn the service into a three-ring circus, a variety hour, a human experience oriented endurance contest. The issue of authentic worship must be addressed. After all, orthodoxy means right praise.

Helmut Thielicke (*Theology of the Spirit*, vol. 3 of *The Evangelical Faith* [Grand Rapids: Eerdmans, 1981], p. 241) has brought the central issues together in these words:

> All ministries and the ministry of all come together in divine service or worship. . . . Worship is twofold. It takes place at a distance from daily life in the form of contemplation and celebration. Its special orientation to Sunday emphasizes this withdrawal even temporally. The gathering for worship is also, however, a departing fellowship which is sent back from celebration into the everyday world with the assurance of continuing fellowship with the Lord. The meditation practiced is worship and triggered by it has the same twofold character. It takes us out of the stress and strain of daily life by way of reflection on what is essential, on the one thing that is fundamentally "needful" in the midst of every necessity or distraction (Luke 10:42). It does this, however, in order that we may be brought back from a sacral distance (that of Sunday worship) to the beginning, middle, and end of our working days.

THE MINISTER MUST PREPARE FOR WORSHIP

How can this rhythmic reality of worship be more genuinely experienced among us? Leitzman has not stated the case too strongly when he observes, "The heart of the Christian life is to be found in the act of public worship." In my upbringing, we were somewhat wary of a printed order of service lest the Holy Spirit be limited. The same logic, of course, has permitted some preachers to come into the pulpit without preparation. The Holy Spirit can as well lead and guide us in effectively planning for the worship service as in the service itself. We can know the Spirit's promptings in the week before as surely as during the actual service. The preparation and planning of the service of worship is imperative.

There is much to be said in favor of building the service around a theme, correlating the Scripture readings, the sermon, the hymns, and the choral music. In some congregations a worship committee works with the pastor and the minister of music in planning the service. Some prayerful, representative participation in planning by laypersons can be helpful. Using laypeople for Scripture reading on occasion and for prayer and testimony introduces meaningful participation. Careful thought given to an attractive order of worship in the bulletin, a more worshipful attitude before the service, and a more sensitive and responsive ministry by the ushers can bring much blessing to the worshiping congregation. Historically, and still in some traditions, there is a concerted effort made to prepare communicants for the Lord's Supper or baptism. The opiate for us all is familiarity. If the observance of the Lord's Supper is not to become mere rote and dull routine, prayerful and skillful preparation needs to be made. Both Matthew Henry and Andrew Murray have written delightful little volumes calculated to be read and studied before coming to Communion. (See Matthew Henry, *The Communicant's Companion* [Glasgow: Chalmers and Collins, 1825]; and Andrew Murray, *The Lord's Table* [New York: Revell, 1897]).

We have all seen notices for the late afternoon cocktail hour posted with the descriptive "Attitude Adjustment Hour." How sad! Think of the opportunity afforded every believer in the remembrance of the Lord Jesus, in fellowship with God and with one another. There is medicine for the soul here, but many times it is perfunctory.

The pastor of the local church faces one of the most exacting and important tasks and privileges in ministry in the leading of worship. The leader of worship needs to prepare his mind and heart. He needs to come to the service fresh, prayed-up, steeped in the riches of Scripture, and filled with the Holy Spirit. There should be nothing hit-and-miss or helter-skelter about the worship service. Nor should he introduce novelty for the sake of novelty, lest attention be turned to the leader rather than to the Lord (C. S. Lewis, *Letters to Malcolm: Chiefly on Prayer* [New York: Harcourt, Brace & World, 1963], p. 4).

The pastor needs to lead key groups in the congregation in serious study of worship. He ought to plumb the great Scriptural classics on the nature and necessity of worship. Historical studies will be of interest to some and can be helpful correctives of overly-idiosyncratic tendencies. Ralph P. Martin's book *Worship in the Early Church* (Westwood, N.J.: Revell, 1964) would be a helpful source. It would be profitable to invite the spiritual leadership of the church to a retreat, using a key book for prior reading. Some books that might be chosen are Ralph P. Martin, *The Worship of God: Some Theological, Pastoral, and Practical Suggestions* (Grand Rapids; Eerdmans, 1982), Robert G. Rayburn, *O Come Let Us Worship: Corporate Worship in the Evangelical Church* (Grand Rapids: Baker, 1980), or, probably most helpful, Paul Waitman Hoon, *The Integrity of Worship* (Nashville,

Tenn.: Abingdon, 1971). A fall series of study-discussions with the college class in our congregation in which we pursued a deeper understanding of aspects of worship was most profitable. During the same season I preached a series of expository messages on "God the Father Almighty," using some of the notable texts in Scripture on the nature and attributes of God. We have almost forgotten the First Person of the Godhead, and, consequently, we have seen the shrinkage of our sense of awe and majesty. We need to think biblical, mind-stretching, great thoughts of God, using the magnificent hymns that are not man-centered and human emotion centered but are truly God-centered. We should work on improving our public reading of the Word of God. We need to use a variety of biblical benedictions. Although we ought not simply to read the prayers, we should seek variety in them from week to week. In all, we need an enlarging sense of the sacred.

Though the pastor is the lead-bird in the flight, so to speak, there is shared leadership. We should have times of analyzing what we are doing. What is meaningful? Why has the sense of mystery eroded in our services? Why has our worship been bleached of a sense of mystery and adoration? Do we have a proper balance between objective and subjective components? Is there a scriptural sense of movement in our worship? Are we appealing to only one personality type? Can we offer more than one track? Are there some options we should consider?

Browne Barr (*High Flying Geese*, p. 40) addressed several of these issues:

> In recent years I have attended public worship in mainline Protestant churches all over the United States and I am appalled by how frequently it feels like an amateur hour. One unattended problem is "pace." The services drag painfully when they most need liveliness, as in prayers and hymns of joy and thanksgiving, and then leap ahead like a frightened deer when we most need time and quietness to confess our limitations or pray in silence. We are shot out of a time of meditation by a vigorous priestly "Amen" before we have had a chance to sense any Holy Presence. Endless fussing with necessary microphones, tedious notices, an announcement by the presider and a long musical introduction by the organist of hymns already posted, choir processionals like traffic jams on a freeway—none of these hindrances could last a month if there were a team atmosphere and candid weekly critiques.

Special attention ought to be given to baptism, infant dedications, weddings, funerals, and other occasional services of the congregation. Each of those services presents unique and exciting opportunities for worship. (William H. Willimon's book, *Worship as Pastoral Care*

[Nashville, Tenn.: Abingdon, 1979] will be a useful source.) There are scriptural and psychological dimensions in each that ought to be thoughtfully weighed and explored. The pastor has a great responsibility in the matter. It is to be hoped that his training, reading, and disposition enable him to address the challenges with wisdom, insight, and courage.

THE BELIEVER MUST PARTICIPATE IN WORSHIP

Worship engages us with the transcendent. It is the reality of God and His Word crashing into our conscious awareness. Worship is human response to the divine initiative. It is more than the pious experience of the human. Too many who attend the services of the church are victims of spectatorism. The essential experience of the football game or the baseball game is transferred to the church service. We come to watch and to listen. We are on the sidelines passively, engrossed but not profoundly engaged. "O come, let us worship the Lord together!" Our worship is to truly renew our minds with the transport of the divine. Folksiness is therefore not the primary goal of the service. It is not to be an ecclesiastical hoedown. What, then, must take place if worship is to be participative?

Concentration on spiritual matters is necessary. Luther long ago observed, "When the Word is active, evil spirits are set in motion." Peter thus advisedly summons us to "Prepare [our] minds for action" (1 Pet. 1:13, NIV). Our minds are tremendously overstimulated; we find it hard to give our attention steadfastly to anything. Before he enters first grade, a six-year-old child in the United States today will have spent 3,000 to 4,000 hours watching television. The high school graduate has spent 15,000 hours before the television compared with 10,800 hours of school time. Paul said, "But one thing I do: Forgetting what is behind and straining toward what is ahead, I press on toward the goal to win the prize for which God has called me heavenward in Christ Jesus" (Phil. 3:13b-14, NIV). Such spiritual concentration is essential for true worship. It is what the dear brother meant who testified, "I woke up this morning with my mind fixed on Jesus!"

The Lord uses different means to get our attention. We live in the din of inequity. We read in the Old Testament of Samuel, "Now Samuel did not yet know the Lord: The word of the Lord had not yet been revealed to him" (1 Sam. 3:7, NIV). The Lord addressed him and he was taught to respond, "Speak, for your servant is listening" (3:10). Are we listening? Our hearts must know time when we are not in the noisy workshop, but in the holy sanctuary. If we are to receive the inner instruction and pass beyond the first stages from knowledge about to acquaintance with, we must learn to center down, to live in the center.

Contemplation of the Lord is necessary. "Looking to Jesus" must be more than a glance, it must be a gaze of the eyes of faith. The cause and effect of this vital focus in worship are set forth in 2 Corinthians 3:18 (NIV), "And we, who with unveiled faces all reflect the Lord's glory, are being transformed into his likeness with ever-increasing glory, which comes from the Lord, who is the Spirit." The essential experience in worship is suggested in 1 Peter 2:4, "As you come to him, the living Stone . . . you also, like living stones, are being built into a spiritual house to be a holy priesthood, offering spiritual sacrifices acceptable to God through Jesus Christ" (NIV). Worship is heart-occupation with the moral excellency and beauty of our Lord and His Word. This is what the narcissism of our time totally misses. George Tyrell, in speaking to another of a man who was much obsessed with his own little problems, remarked, "He does not look at the stars enough." That essential focus opens the low ceiling and gives us glimpses of the light beyond. It is a lifelong vista for the believer. Charles Kingsley's dying words were, "How beautiful God is!"

Consecration of the heart is necessary. The pattern for the believer's activity as represented by Jesus is both a coming in and a going out (John 10:9). There is an important relationship between our worship and our work. The rhythmic lifting up of heart and mind to Christ will make dedicated service possible and effective. Out of that deep impression comes vital expression. The psalmist intimates something of this relationship when he says, "And let the beauty of the Lord our God be upon us: and establish thou the work of our hands upon us" (Ps. 90:17, KJV). Professor William E. Hocking penetrated the heart of the matter when he observed, "The soul over-steeped in actual work loses capacity to believe in the presence of the good worked for," though, in turn, "worship cannot last — when too prolonged it becomes automatic and mechanical." He therefore urges an alternating current, citing the old Egyptian proverb "The archer hitteth the target, partly by pulling, partly by letting go; the boatman reacheth the landing, partly by pulling, partly by letting go" (*The Meaning of God in Human Experience* [New Haven: Yale University Press, 1912]). Worship "in spirit and in truth" eventuates in obedient response and action. The Cure of Arns asked a peasant why he came into the church to meditate. The answer was: "Jesus looks at me and I look at Him." That is worship.

THE PREACHING AND TEACHING OF THE WORD OF GOD ENLARGES THE MIND

Preaching has a unique place in God's plan and in Christian worship. The apostle is unequivocal in his insistence: "And at his appointed season he brought his word to light through the preaching entrusted to me by the command of God our Savior" (Titus 1:3, NIV). Although many Christians have personal and private study and reading programs, a greater number look to the public communication of God's Word for their essential nourishment and spiritual feeding. That means that the pastor cannot rest satisfied with Sunday supplement or *Reader's Digest* preaching, which serves up various materials of passing interest with small doses of substance. One of the greatest needs in the contemporary battle for the mind is a mighty renewal of powerful biblical preaching, rich and scriptural in content, practical and for life today in its impact.

THE CRISIS IN PULPIT COMMUNICATION

On the whole there seems to be a rather low view of preaching in the land. Webster's *Third New International Dictionary* indicates as much in one of the definitions it gives of preaching: "To exhort in an officious and tiresome manner." People say with exasperation: "Now, don't preach at me!" Part of the problem about our seeming lack of great preaching is our lack of great listening. We do not have much of what Aaron Copeland calls "talented listening." CEBU (continuously exposed but unverified) is the nightmare in the television business. People hear so much that they effectively register very little.

Some preaching is like speaking into a dead microphone. There is an information overload. H. H. Farmer has well reminded us that preaching is a unique form—it is not an essay, a discussion, or a lecture. The preacher must not be content with stating what is true. He must be dedicated to communicating what is true. Some sermons are weighty and factual but have about as much spark as a load of wet cement. We need more than information; we need illumination and inspiration. Most young preachers attempt too much in their preaching. One or two main ideas carefully and prayerfully developed are about what should be attempted. After all, as Ruskin observed, we have thirty minutes in the sermon in which to raise the dead! Pulpit fog does not help in the life which is fighting a hard battle. Mono-mood discourse offers little for the breaking heart. John Wycliffe offered good advice when he said: "The preacher should preach appropriately, simply, directly, and from a devout and sincere heart."

A poor woman said of a preacher in Thomas Guthrie's days, "He's neither edifyin' nor divertin'," and the same could be said of some today. Strangely enough, some who have a high view of Scripture seem to have a low view of preaching, at least that is the conclusion suggested by the amount of time and effort they give to the preparation of the message from the Word. A. T. Robertson felt that some obviously appear to put their minds to rest when they preach. All is dullness and blandness. The preacher becomes "a master of echoes." "He's a good preacher," the Scot said, "he's a right harmless laddie." Why is it that some sermons seem to be an invitation to check the mind at the door rather than a summons for the Word to break loose with its tingling, gripping, searing power? So much preaching seems to lack the vital wattage of the Spirit's enabling. Thinking is hard work in church as anywhere else, but it must be axiomatic for the preacher: Engage brain before opening mouth. The sermon must be more than articulate snoring.

We may feel we have slender apparatus. That is the glory of the cracked jug, and but casts us in a deeper dependence upon the Lord. Sibbes stammered, Liddon and Surgeon were victims of melancholy, Manning had his sniffs and snorts in preaching, George Morrison a non-carrying voice, A. T. Robertson a slight hesitation in speech. The critical necessity is not so much for brilliant gifts as it is for hearts and minds alive and aglow. Wordsworth argued that what comes from the heart goes to the heart. I like Picasso's aim: "I want to draw the mind in the direction it's not used to and wake it up!" "Give me your convictions, not your doubts," Goethe demanded. The sermon ought to come like Eve from somewhere near the third rib, with the heart still beating. Or as Richard Baxter testified, "I preached as never sure to preach again, and as a dying man to dying men."

THE CONTENT OF PULPIT COMMUNICATION

Vital and relevant preaching must be biblical preaching. Too long or too thin servings of the Word of God will not suffice. The text of Scripture is to be more than a motto over the sermon. The Bible is to be far more than the source of the opening quotation in the sermon. Of some sermons it could be said, if the text had scarlet fever the sermon would never catch it. It is the pallid and pulpy content of sermons that leaves the flock unfed and unstimulated. We need exposition of Scripture, not the imposition of our own pet ideas and hobbies. It is, after all, the Word itself that saves, not our comment on the Word.

Epochal preaching is biblical preaching. We are not called to serve up carved cherry pits but the living Word of God! The meaning of the passage is not ours to decide but ours to discover. Some preachers are in their anecdotage. The skyscraper sermon consists of one story after another. James Daane wisely warns against the shish kebob skewer sermon—alternating pieces of meat and anecdote. That is canned preaching. Though it is hard to find fresh illustrations, the preacher should remember that every aspect of the art and science and craft of preaching is hard work.

We need strong content in our preaching today that will leave neither the mind or the heart untouched. So many sermons are like summer lightening—they flash all over but do not really strike anywhere. The mysterious, creative power of the Word is breathtaking. People are hungry for the Word. There is a great vacuum in the modern mind that is without God. We are not a wise people. Gabriel Marcel has well chronicled *The Decline of Wisdom* (Philosophical Library, 1955). We have in our hands that Word of God "which is able to make [us] wise unto salvation" (2 Tim. 3:15, KJV). That is what we need to share.

CONSIDERATIONS FOR BETTER PULPIT COMMUNICATION

Practitioners of preaching need to target specific areas for continual effort and attention if they are to escape an incessant chopping of straw.

Strong use of language. Sometimes our sermons are a verbal souffle. We are victims of our verbicide. Inescapably we are vendors of words—a sermon is a treasury of words. We face the serious devaluation of our verbal currency. We need to pursue the right words—not always the pretty words or the poetic words, but the right words. We need the words that are clear and cogent and compelling. We need a more athletic pronunciation of the words we choose. Preachers never graduate from language school.

Imagination. Beuchner defines imagination as "conjuring up inside one, by use of a very specific intellectual muscle, that which is absent or elusive by making it concrete." Concreteness in preaching must be cultivated. Joseph Conrad aptly observed, "The stuff that comes easy is dull reading." We need to do the kind of reading and creative brooding that brings new things into being. Freshness is the need of the hour.

Preaching for a verdict. It was said of Donald McIntosh that he was "always preaching for a verdict." We are weakest today in application and conclusion. Sermons tend to sag toward the end. There is little sense of the climactic. We need to work on "preaching it home."

Preaching without notes. Television makes the use of notes and manuscripts unthinkable. They are an effective barricade to communication. The sermon must be a knock on the door. Each person in

Whitefield's audience felt as though the message was for him and him alone. Thus H. H. Farmer in *The Servant of the Word* (Nisbet & Co., 1942) argued that reading the sermon muffles the significant personal relationship. We need oral not written style.

Preaching in expository series. We nudge our hearers into more significant study when we pursue balanced expository series. Sometimes the series should be microscopic, and sometimes it should be panoramic. We need to get a good blend of Old Testament, gospel, and epistolary involvement. The worship service is a tremendously challenging hour for the expositor of Scripture.

THE COMPLEMENTS OF PULPIT COMMUNICATION

What is done in the pulpit to engage the minds and hearts of men and women must be in a context of significant and effective interpersonal relationships. What the preacher is and what he does are as important as what he says. In the interests of enhancing the pulpit ministry in terms of relationships, I would like to offer some specific suggestions:

Foster dialogue. The preaching event is more dialogical than many suppose if we are experiencing the inspiration of the Spirit and if we are interacting with our congregation in that extraordinary reality of spiritual flow. We need to supplement dialogue, however, in the interests of deeper interaction. During the more provocative series, such as those on the Ten Commandments, or during a problem series on insistent and inescapable interrogatives, I have used a sermon talk-back procedure on Sunday evenings. After the evening service, interested friends could come down to the fellowship hall for light refreshments and an open-mike opportunity to raise issues and interact with the preacher. In several pastorates these evenings have proved to be valuable times of sharing. There are those in the congregation who want to probe more deeply and who want to raise questions that perhaps the preacher chose to ignore in the sermon. Some parishioners see the pulpit as the coward's castle. Open-mike questioning of the pastor becomes an opportunity to get beyond any starched rhetoric to the real heart of the matter.

Encourage sharing. Too often our preaching and teaching are pitched to the lowest common denominator. Certainly we should have special education classes in our Christian education enterprise. Also, we should target the gifted student and not encourage boredom and a premature checkout. Some of our high school students are studying Russian and are taking in all kinds of advanced and enriched courses. In several parishes, I have arranged for study-discussion groups in elective classes during the Sunday school hour. Some quarters I would offer classes on the great Christian classics, limiting the number of participants to twenty per class. We have tackled Christianity and mental health, and also readings in contemporary theology or Ecclesiastes, raising in this last the question of whether or not the pursuit of happiness is a wild goose chase. Not all of the courses would be of general interest, but there are those who by temperament and disposition have an interest. They can be encouraged and challenged by something a little more formidable, and the preacher in turn can get additional soundings from his flock.

WHERE WE STAND

The preservation of a truly Christian biblical mind-set in our time is an awesome and formidable challenge. Powerful secular and even demonic ideologies pervade our culture and press in relentlessly upon the conscious and unconscious minds of young and old. We Christians have conformed to the thought patterns and mores of the present evil age to a greater extent than we may recognize. The alternative to the capitulation of the Christian mind to these forces is for the Christian to be "transformed by the renewing of [his] mind" (Rom. 12:2, NIV).

Fortunately, in minding our minds, we are not entirely on our own. The New Testament principle is clear: "For none of us lives to himself alone" (Rom., 14:7, NIV). We need each other. The unique spiritual community called the church is not only a bastion of defense against evil incursion, but is a base for the mounting of a powerful and effective challenge upon "the gates of hell" (Matt. 16:18, KJV).

As part of the church of Jesus Christ, Christians not only participate in a corporate witness for the truth of God in the battle for the mind, but they minister to each other positively and practically in the bonds of spiritual affection and understanding. From the standpoint of the individual, the family, the local Christian community, the nation, and the peoples of global village, the corporate and collective experience of God's people is focal and central. "Thanks be to God who gives *us* the victory through our Lord Jesus Christ!"

6 Devotions and the Spirit-Controlled Mind

Grant Osborne

Dear Sir:

I am writing in response to your request for additional information. In block #3 of the accident reporting form, I put quote—LOST PRESENCE OF MIND—unquote as the cause of my accident. You said in your letter that I should explain more fully, and I trust that the following details will be sufficient.

I am a bricklayer by trade. On the day of the accident, I was working alone on the roof of a six-story building. When I completed my work, I discovered that I had about 500 lbs. of brick left over. Rather than carry the bricks down by hand, I decided to lower them in a barrel by using a pulley which fortunately was attached to the side of the building at the sixth floor.

Securing the rope at ground level, I went up to the roof, swung the barrel out, and loaded the bricks into it. Then I went back to the ground and untied the rope, holding it tightly to insure a slow descent of the 500 lbs. of bricks. You will note in block #11 of the accident reporting form that I weigh 135 lbs.

Due to my surprise at being jerked off the ground so suddenly, *I lost my presence of mind* and forgot to let go of the rope. Needless to say I proceeded at a rather rapid rate up the side of the building.

In the vicinity of the third floor, I met the barrel coming down. This explains the fractured skull and broken collarbone.

Slowed only slightly, I continued my rapid ascent, not stopping until the fingers of my right hand were two-knuckles deep into the pulley.

Fortunately, by this time I had regained my *presence of mind* and was able to hold tightly to the rope in spite of my pain.

At approximately the same time, however, the barrel of bricks hit the ground — and the bottom fell out of the barrel. Devoid of the weight of the bricks, the barrel now weighed approximately 50 lbs.

I refer you again to my weight in block #11. As you might imagine, I began a rapid descent down the side of the building. In the vicinity of the third floor, I met the barrel coming up. This accounts for the two fractured ankles and the lacerations of my legs and lower body.

This encounter with the barrel slowed me enough to lessen my injuries when I fell into the pile of bricks and, fortunately, only three vertebrae were cracked.

I am sorry to report, however, that as I lay there on the bricks — in pain, unable to stand, and watching the empty barrel six stories above me — I again *lost presence of mind* — I let go the rope.*

Many Christians today would identify with the theme of this fictitious (and anonymous) letter, "Lost Presence of Mind." It is extremely difficult to maintain a Christian way of thinking when we are continually tugged this way and that by the enticing messages of our culture. One of the most famous quotes from Pogo is applicable: "We have met the enemy, and he is us." How do we regain a mode of thought that can function as an antidote to the pneumonia of secularity? How can we find the "presence of mind" that can help us to fight the forces assaulting our Christian lives? It is the transforming presence of the Holy Spirit within (Rom. 12:2) that will enable us to fend off the world-forces arrayed against us and to go on the offensive (2 Cor. 10:4–5; Eph. 6:10–12).

In our offensive and defensive strategies we should rely on two sources of spiritual support: (1) our church, through corporate worship and fellowship, to provide us with counter information to jam the propaganda machine of paganism, and (2) our devotional life, to help us keep open direct communion with the mind of God.

In his essay David Larsen described the resources of the church for the believer. In this essay I would like to propose that a proper experience of Bible study and prayer will enable the believer to tap the mind

*Source unknown.

of God and to alter the mental paths into which the non-Christian world may sometimes lead him. Christians face a major problem: they receive too much of their mental input from the world and too little from biblical sources. Up to 90 percent of the information they sort in their minds is controlled by presuppositions antithetical to a Christian viewpoint. Therefore they must increase the amount of time spent in genuine, rich fellowship with other Christians, and they must work for better experiences in their devotional life.

Devotions means, of course, that experience which increases a person's love for and communion with God. The word comes from the term *devote*, defined in *Webster's Dictionary* as a solemn act of dedication involving the giving up of one's self wholly and the centering of one's attention completely on the other. The noun refers to "religious fervor," especially in "an act of prayer or supplication." The term therefore means that the major purpose of our devotional activity is not so much winning God to our side or asking Him to do something for us as it is our act of piety, the aligning of ourselves with God. Tom Smail, in "Life in the Holy Spirit" (*The Lion Handbook of Christian Belief,* ed. Robin Keeley [Herts, England: Lion Publishing, 1982], p. 370), observes that

> Christian prayer rightly understood is not a do-it-yourself activity, a matter of finding the right techniques to reach God and bring him our requests. . . . The first priority in prayer therefore is not to ask. It is rather to listen to see how the Spirit is going to prompt us to pray, to discover from him for whom and for what we ought to be asking.

In other words, the prime mover in both prayer and Bible study is God. We seek His input and direction for our lives.

The further purpose of a significant devotional life is to align our thought life with God's ways. Francis Schaeffer argues in "Freedom in the Thought Life" (*True Spirituality* [Wheaton, Ill.: Tyndale, 1971], pp. 120-22) that the determining factor in one's life is not external actions but internal thoughts. The internal causes and controls the external. He draws three conclusions: (1) the reality of loving communion with God must occur in the inner self; the priority must always be to love God "with all my heart and soul and mind"; (2) the real battle takes place in the world of ideas, "conventional ideas internally acted upon"; (3) true spirituality must begin in our thought-world, and it is there that the spiritual battle is won or lost. It should be added that the battle for the mind must begin in vital communion with God in Bible study and prayer.

Although in one sense both Bible study and prayer are God-oriented, in another sense they form a two-way street of our spiritual communion with the Lord. It is in Bible study that God speaks to us, while in prayer we speak to Him. Both perspectives are valid and interdependent. In fact, neither is complete without the other. Bible study provides the content, and prayer the active trust for the Christian life.

BIBLE STUDY: THE MIND'S CONTENT

We live in an age when communication techniques are multiplying with dazzling speed. Dick Tracy's television wristwatch is already a reality, and high-tech computers are bringing whole libraries into our homes. Futurists are predicting the time when the Library of Congress will be on-line and ready to be tapped for instant information. Yet, though information has never been more accessible, true communication has never seemed more distant. The Me-generation attitude has made people feel isolated, without a friend in the world. Even in the church it has become difficult to overcome such a mind-set.

An information revolution has affected what we can learn about the Bible. There is more information on biblical background and word studies than ever before. A great number of excellent Bible commentaries, dictionaries, and encyclopedias make that material available to the general public. Yet for many Christians, the Bible has ceased being living literature: the excitement of Bible study has departed and has been replaced by a lethargic "I-study-it-because-I'm-supposed-to-as-a-Christian" attitude. This lack of enthusiasm for Bible study has awesome consequences. J. I. Packer in the foreword to R. C. Sproul, *Knowing Scripture* (Downers Grove, Ill.: InterVarsity, 1977), pp. 7–10, says: "If I were the devil . . . I should broadcast doubts about the truths and relevance and good sense and straightforwardness of the Bible. . . . At all costs I should want to keep them from using their minds in a disciplined way to get the measure of its message." How can there be a reawakening of interest in the kind of Bible study that leads us to worship, to bow down in adoration to God, to sense the majesty and awesomeness of El Shaddai? Christians need to ask the Holy Spirit to open their minds so that once again they might sense the power, comfort, and beauty of God's Word.

Evidently some Christians are doing just that. We see a renewed interest in lay Bible study. Christians from various backgrounds are beginning to search the Scriptures (Acts 17:11). The results of that search are startling. A true study of the Scriptures takes the student into God's very presence. As he sees the personal involvement and compassion of the Creator of the Universe for His creatures, his heart should be filled with wonder; as he senses his calling to be among

God's special people, he should be humbled. As he sees the Lord's justice and His demands for radical discipleship, he should be moved to ask the Lord for strength. And his study also should be exciting for him as he recognizes how great a source of spiritual power is available to help him live the Christian life.

To draw up a complete compendium of these themes through biblical literature is impossible in a short essay. Consequently, this essay will focus on the principles that can be learned from Joshua's experience of walking with God. In the first chapter of Joshua, we see that Joshua faced many of the same problems you and I confront, including feelings of inadequacy. As a military man, he had been asked to fill Moses' shoes and feels that he cannot. Three times in vv. 5–9 God said,"Be strong and courageous," and twice He added, "I will be with you" (all NIV). In v. 8 God gave Joshua a "formula" for success. I call this formula the "three R's" of the Christian walk.

READ THE BIBLE

"You will never stop mentioning this Book of the Law" is a literal rendition of the first clause of Joshua 1:8. It means to go over and over God's prescriptive laws, to memorize them. Yet this is more than mere rote memorization, for it presupposes the action which follows. The "Book of the Law" (NIV) is linked to the whole destiny of Israel. At the entrance to the Promised Land it was read antiphonally on Mount Gerizim and Mount Ebal (Josh. 8:34). Yet the nation forgot the law and vacillated between adherence and apostasy. The extent to which the "Book of the Law" was central determined the blessings of Yahweh upon the land. When it was rediscovered by Josiah (2 Kings 22:8, 11) revival occurred. It was soon forgotten, however. The resultant apostasy led to the exile. Again the "Book of the Law" was found by Ezra (Neh. 8:3), and the last vestiges of idolatry were destroyed.

Israel, like Christians today, had to learn that her future depended upon the contents of her thinking. Would the divinely revealed "Book" or her pagan neighbors determine her attitudes and actions? With which "Book" would she spend her time? God was not asking Joshua for a casual attitude toward the Book of the Law but for a definite commitment to give it priority.

God calls us to a commitment to His Word. The barrier to such commitment is seldom laziness; for most of us it is lack of motivation. We know we should study the Bible but just do not quite seem to get around to it. One man said to me recently, "I just am not a reader; I never pick up books or even newspapers. I'm an action person." I found out that his hobby was restoring antiques, and I noticed an entire shelf of works addressed to the topic. I pointed to the shelf, "Oh, sure," he said, "but I don't read them. I consult them." "Why?" I asked. "I have to so that I use the proper technique and know the value of what I am working on." "Why, that is exactly what the Bible does," I responded. "It gives us principles for living. If it is not consulted regularly, we will make the wrong choices. Our values will be all mixed up."

One reason many of us lack a desire to have a meaningful devotional life is the widespread impression that we should just read a chapter and then pray. Such a cursory reading, accomplished in just a few minutes, rarely thrills the soul. Even more important, it fails to provide the alternate mind-set that can combat secular control of our thought processes. Too frequently, we follow this approach: (1) grit the teeth in disciplining ourselves to read Scripture; (2) disengage the mind; and (3) start reading. If we have to force ourselves to do something, it is proof positive we are not experiencing joy in doing it.

I challenge the reader: Make the Word your hobby. In saying that, I am not denigrating the Bible. A hobby is something one wants to engage in, and it is something one is willing to spend time learning how to do. I am asking you to spend thirty to forty minutes a day studying the Word. Many of us spend more time than that reading the newspaper. The difficulty is rearranging our hectic schedules. Yet we are willing to do just that for an extra tennis lesson or an evening of bowling league games. It is a matter of priorities. In a valuable book, *Work, Play, and Worship in a Leisure-Oriented Society* (Minneapolis: Aubsburg, 1972), Gordon Dahl has argued that Americans worship their work, work at their play, and play at their worship. We must correct the imbalance and demonstrate that the Lord, not the world, has control of our minds.

The inductive method is an important tool for meaningful Bible study. In it, the reader seeks to delineate the major theme(s) and development of thought in a book or a passage. The method demands that the student work from a paragraph Bible, and indeed such a version of the Bible is a crucial corrective to one barrier to understanding Scripture, the verse divisions. The Bible was not divided into chapters and verses until 1551 when a Parisian publisher, Stephanus, did it over several months on a trip publicizing his latest edition of the Greek New Testament. Tradition would have us believe that he accomplished part of his task while riding on his horse, some divisions resulting from his pen's being constantly jostled. Whatever the truth of that account, we ought not to separate the verses from their context, but instead should interpret any sentence in light of the larger paragraph.

In the inductive study, the first step is to chart the entire book. That can be done in several steps. A sheet of paper should be marked off into columns. Then the paragraphs of the biblical text should be skimmed and the contents summarized on the sheet of paper. Next, the student should look for developing patterns in the book and reorganize his notes according to those patterns; that is, he should note major shifts of thought and major emphases. Consider the book of Revelation.

What one notices immediately is that the book jumps back and forth from scenes in heaven (chaps. 1; 4-5; 7; 10; 14) to scenes on earth (chaps. 2-3; 6; 8-9; 11-13; 15-18). Furthermore, the basic themes of the scenes are contrasted: the chaos and agony on earth set over against the joy and worship in heaven. A primary theme unites the scenes: the sovereignty of God and the futility of Satan. That is an exciting message of comfort, and it can be unlocked by a simple chart-study of the book. God is indeed in control of history, and His enemies (and ours) are doomed to final judgment, no matter how powerful they seem at present.

The student should also chart the smaller unit, the paragraph. Here he can use sentences as the basic building blocks. For this task, the most useful Bible version will probably be the *New American Standard Bible,* because it closely reproduces the original languages. The main clauses will usually carry the major thought, and the other clauses will carry clarifying ideas. Then the student should chart the developing pattern of the major thoughts. Soon he will have discovered the basic message of the paragraph. For instance, Col. 3:1-4 has three main thoughts: seek things above, think things above, and you will appear with Him in glory. Because the first two thoughts are synonymous, there are actually only two major ideas in the passage, a command (think about and seek heavenly rather than earthly things) and a promise (God will give us a share in Jesus' glory at the Eschaton). The basic theme is the importance of keeping one's mind fixed on spiritual rather than fleshly pursuits.

REFLECT UPON THE BIBLE

As Joshua memorizes the book of the law, he must "meditate on it day and night" (Josh. 1:8). Meditation is an important part of the devotional life. Edmund Clowney (*CM: Christian Meditation* [Nutley, N.J.: Craig Press, 1979], p. 41) writes, "Too often, through lack of meditation, Christians become secularized and their capacity to see the world before the Lord shrivels," and he suggests "a focused seeing, a contemplative examination of both the richness and reality of . . . God's works." It is critical to understand that in Scripture to meditate does not mean to muse upon Scripture in terms of the application of a passage to any area of life we wish. It is just the opposite. The ancient rabbis would mutter the Scriptures to themselves in order to understand what the text actually said. In an excellent article on meditation in Scripture, "God's Directives for His Work" (*Christianity Today* 3, no. 7 [5 January 1959], pp. 12-13), H. C. Leupold notes that there are four doctrines in Joshua 1:6-9: (1) Go forward strong in the faith of God's promises, (2) direct your course by the Word, (3) live in the sacred oracles of God, (4) trust in the Lord's presence. One meditates on Scripture when he does a thoughtful Bible study. That does not mean that the classical sense of meditation, the deep reflection upon spiritual realities, should be disparaged. It is indeed critical for a proper walk with God. But the meditation spoken of in Joshua 1:8 is actually the study of meaning. In it the student asks what God is saying in His laws.

There are dangers in meditation. One is to read into the text what we want it to mean, a practice called eisegesis. The aim instead should be to draw out of the text what it actually means, or to practice exegesis. The other danger is to read twentieth-century meanings into ancient terms. The one who meditates on Scripture needs to remember that God revealed His truths in human language that spoke to peoples of ancient cultures. Because it is important for us to understand the culture within which the original message was couched as we try to discern its meaning, and because today we have no intuitive grasp of the biblical culture, excellent study tools are essential. They might include a good Bible dictionary (e.g., *New Bible Dictionary* or *New Unger's Bible Dictionary*), a concordance (Strong's or Young's; the NASB concordance), background books (Daniel-Rops, *Daily Life in the Time of Jesus;* or Osborne and Liefeld, *Manners and Customs in Bible Lands* [forthcoming, Moody Press]), and commentaries (the Tyndale or the Laymen's commentary sets).

In seeking the meaning of a text, the major criterion to use is context. New Testament interpretations must always fit the first-century setting and the developing ideas of the larger context in which the passage is placed. For example, 2 Timothy 2:15, which in the KJV begins "Study to show thyself approved unto God" is frequently misused to support Bible memorization. The New King James Version correctly translates it, "Be diligent to present yourselves approved to God."[1] The translation stresses the need for zeal in following God's demands, so that one

---

1. From *The New King James Version.* Copyright © 1979, 1980, 1982, Thomas Nelson, Inc., Publishers.

might become "a worker who does not need to be ashamed." Agricultural imagery appears earlier in the chapter (v. 6), and from it we sense in v. 15 an allusion to the day laborer the farmer hires, whose work must meet high standards if he is to be kept on the job. The agricultural background is relevant, also, to the last phrase of v. 15, "rightly dividing the word of truth," which could be paraphrased, "plowing a straight furrow through the word of truth." Our devotional life, then, is dependent upon our discovery of the actual message of Scripture. Using tools such as dictionaries and commentaries will help us overcome our lack of knowledge of the milieu within which a passage is placed.

Deuteronomy 6:6-9 is another passage illustrating the importance and the process of Bible study:

> And these words, which I am commanding you today, shall be on your heart; and you shall teach them diligently to your sons and shall talk of them when you sit in your house and when you walk by the way and when you lie down and when you rise up. And you shall bind them as a sign on your hand and they shall be as frontals on your forehead. And you shall write them on the doorposts of your house and on your gates.

The passage illustrates the overriding importance of the Word of God. It follows the Shema (Deut. 6:4-5), the basic creed of the Jews. Study of the Word, then, was to be central in every area of Jewish life. The language of vv. 8-9 was meant to be imagery, but the Jews took it literally. They made phylacteries, little pouches containing parchment on which were written Exodus 13:1-16; and Deuteronomy 6:4-9; 11:13-20. These they wore on the forehead and wrist, even as late as the time of Christ. The mezuzah, a similar pouch placed on the doorpost, was created to fulfill v. 9. In the context, however, vv. 6-9 meant that the Word of God must be primary in every aspect of the life of the people of God. R. C. Sproul says, "Here God sovereignly commands that his Word be taught so diligently that it penetrates the heart. The content of that Word is not to be mentioned casually and infrequently. Repeated discussion is the order of the day, everyday" (*Knowing Scripture*, p. 20).

REACT TO THE BIBLE

The purpose of memorization and meditation upon the Law as described in Joshua 1:8 was that Joshua (and the people of God in every generation) might "be careful to do according to all that is written in it." What good would there be for Joshua to learn the Law if he did not heed it! The climax of Joshua 1:6–9 is in this clause, for it tells how Joshua can align himself with the victorious presence of God. In fact, the two final statements, "for then you will make your way prosperous and have good success"[2] build upon the earlier command to meditate on the law. Although in one sense the statements are synonymous, they do present the two sides of biblical success: as a result of heeding God's commands, Joshua would "make" his own way "prosperous," and also God would bless his way and guarantee "success." The heart of devotional Bible study occurs here. The Word of God is not merely an academic book to be studied; it is a life-oriented book meant to change lives. If we fail to apply the Word of God to our daily situations, we have short-circuited our study of the life-giving Word.

A short-circuited approach to the Bible has numerous drawbacks. Roy B. Zuck notes that it "reduces God's Word to a mere object or antique museum piece to be examined by scientific inquiry, relegates Bible study to an academic exercise, and restricts the Scriptures to being only a sourcebook of information with little regard for its life-changing relevance" ("Application in Biblical Hermeneutics and Exposition," in *Walvoord: A Tribute,* ed. Donald K. Campbell [Chicago: Moody, 1982], p. 15). Zuck defines application as "the process of communicating the present-day relevance of a biblical text, specifying how that relevance may be translated into action, and inviting and urging the hearers to make that transference" ("Application," p. 19). Yet the process is by its very nature a complex one. Walter Liefeld discusses the two foci, either of which is dangerous if taken alone: (1) the approach "from above," from the inspired text itself, can ignore the actual situation of the congregation and thus seem lifeless; (2) the approach "from below," from the needs of the congregation, can ignore the original meaning of the text. "The former method leads to irrelevance; the latter, to distortion" (*New Testament Exposition: From Text to Sermon* [Grand Rapids: Zondervan, 1984], p. 95). Our task in devotional Bible study is to wed the two, text to context, so that the text of Scripture speaks to the needs of our present condition.

In seeking the middle ground in which the original horizon of the biblical passage is joined to the contemporary horizon of the present life-situation, the Christian performs the task of interpretation. Because devotion has as its task a spiritual response to God, it includes both worship and obedient conduct. Berkeley Mickelson speaks of five goals

---

2. From *The New King James Version.* Copyright © 1979, 1980, 1982, Thomas Nelson, Inc., Publishers.

of personal Bible study: (1) fellowship with God through the Scriptures, as believers listen to what God has to say in the text, (2) directions from God for the decisions of life, as Christians respond in both major and minor crises to the guidance of Scripture by maintaining an awareness of God's presence and an openness to His will, (3) commands of God for daily living, as saints obey the direct injunctions of God's Word, (4) the counsel of God for personal dialogue, as Christians share their faith with others, and (5) the message of God for public preaching, as the pastor confronts others with the demands that have gripped his own life (*Interpreting the Bible* [Grand Rapids: Eerdmans, 1963], pp. 345-66).

There are four steps to a proper application. First, we must determine the original situation and message of the text. That is discovered by applying the background material to the problems addressed in the passage, and then determining the situation behind the biblical injunctions. For instance, 1 Corinthians 11:2-16 has long been interpreted as an assertion by Paul that women should be veiled. But James Hurley, in *Men and Women in Biblical Perspective* (Grand Rapids: Zondervan, 1981), pages 254-71, argues cogently that something else may be meant by the passage. In the ancient world honorable women did not allow their hair to flow loose; such was the practice only of prostitutes. Thus, though women had a new equality with men (see Gal. 3:28), it was appropriate for them to surrender to the leadership of their husbands and to wear their hair properly. Anything less would have been disgraceful to outsiders and a denial of the divinely-bestowed order.

Second, we should consider the underlying theological principle behind the text. What was Paul's argument as he addressed the problem in Corinth? It is clear that Paul used the argument from creation (vv. 8-9) for the wife's submission to her husband. It is also clear that throughout the passage there are strong cultural overtones in the language: "disgrace" (v. 6), "proper" (v. 13), "contentious" (v. 16), "no other wisdom" (v. 16) (all NIV). This language plus the distance between Paul's theological argument and the cultural situation leads most scholars to conclude that the admonition concerning the way the Corinthian women wore their hair was designed to meet a specific cultural problem rather than to serve as a teaching of universal applicability.

Third, we should meditate on the biblical and theological truths studied. That will require solitude and a willingness to think through clearly the implications of the passage. Contemplation is an attempt to draw near to God and involves not the emptying of the mind (as in TM) but the conscious stretching of the mind towards God. It is best to focus upon a particular aspect of God or His revelation. Often study of a particular passage provides a perfect opportunity for deep meditation. In actuality the process bridges the second and fourth steps. We ask ourselves, "How can these spiritual truths speak to my situation?"

Fourth, the reader should seek to discern parallels between the original situation addressed by a Biblical writer and the contemporary experiences of the church. It is at this level that application should occur. Again, the important thing to recall is that the parallels should be genuine ones. The question we should ask is this: "If the biblical writer were exhorting my church on this topic, what phases of church life would he address?" At the same time we must know ourselves and the world in which we live. Introspection and broad reading will help in that. We need to search ourselves honestly, noting dark areas where the light of the Word must shine. We need to examine our relationships with others, so that we can bring the Word of God to shine upon community life. Finally, we need to understand our changing world by reading newsmagazines and timely books. Overall, we need to bring the Word of God to bear on our own analysis of the current world scene. The spotlight of the Word of God should cast light into the nooks and crannies of our own soul, and its searching beam should be cast upon a world that is in darkness.

A further example of drawing parallels can be demonstrated by referring to the letter to the church of Laodicea in Revelation 3:14-22. There the Lord takes note of three things for which Laodicea was famed—its banking, its garment industry, and its eye salve—to show its spiritual deprivation. The Lord takes note also of something Laodicea lacked—water that was definitely cold, as was Colossae's, or definitely hot, as was Hierapolis's—to indicate how distasteful the immaturity of the Laodiceans was. The underlying principle is God's displeasure with a self-centered, success-oriented church. The parallels with today's churches are quite plain—those areas in which modern Western Christians take pride. Each of us has areas in our life where self rather than God rules, where we seek the plaudits of our peers rather than to please God.

Zuck ("Application," pp. 26-36) says of the application of a passage that it must (1) be based on a "principlizing bridge" between the narrative and the audience that is inherent in the meaning yet applicable to today, (2) be based on elements common to the original setting and the current reader, (3) result in specific action or response.[3]

---

3. I should like to thank my colleague Dr. Charles Sell for valuable comments concerning this subject.

SUMMATION ON BIBLE STUDY

At first glance it may appear that we are making a very complex process out of devotional Bible study. However, we are not charting successive steps but rather are describing simultaneous processes with which to do serious Bible study. Nor are we denying the value of Scripture reading programs. They are valuable supplements to detailed study. But broad reading can never become an end in itself. The only way to train the mind to think biblically is to keep it in deep biblical thoughts.

Practically speaking, I would suggest the following approach. Take ruled, lined paper and divide it into three columns. From the red line to the left edge write the text. Use two-thirds of the remainder to discuss the meaning of the text and the other third to apply it to your life. Place prayers in the third column, which will then become specific requests in your time of supplication. For instance, for Philippians 4:6 you might write, "Be anxious for nothing." Then you can note that this means, "Stop worrying about anything," and that there is a parallel reference to materialism in Matthew 6:25-34. In the third column you might write, "Lord, help me not to worry about my car payment. May I learn to trust you more than my ability to make money."

PRAYER: THE MIND'S COMMUNICATION

Charles Swindoll (*Encourage Me: Caring Words for Heavy Hearts* [Portland, Oreg.: Multnomah, 1982], pp. 42-43) tells the story of an airplane that at the end of an uneventful flight suddenly refused to engage the landing wheels. In that deceptively calm voice so often used, the pilot explained the situation to the passengers step-by-step as he tried to coax the wheels down. Finally, with the runway covered with foam, he told the passengers to place their heads between their knees and hold onto their ankles. He concluded his directions with this announcement: "We are beginning our final descent. At this moment, in accordance with International Aviation Codes established at Geneva, it is my obligation to inform you that if you believe in God you should commence prayer." The belly landing was perfect.

Prayer is one of the most difficult areas of the Christian life. On the one hand it involves communion with God, yet on the other hand the very concept is a matter of faith. Prayer often seems like a monologue. In our society it is difficult enough to communicate with one's spouse and friends, let alone with the invisible God. We can all identify with the problem of Peter. Speaking of Christ, he writes, "Whom having not seen, ye love; in whom, though now ye see him not, yet believing, ye rejoice with joy unspeakable and full of glory" (1 Pet. 1:8, KJV). We have not seen Him and do not see Him; prayer is an act of love, done in faith, and only then can result in the joy that cannot be shaken, enabling us to participate in the divine glory.

Jacques Ellul (*Prayer and Modern Man,* trans. C. Edward Hopkin [New York: Seabury, 1970], p. 140) argues that prayer can be nothing but combat in this age of alienation when truth is sacrificed to the god of relevance. This is a time "in which man gives rein to every presumption and experiences every terror. It is a time in which our wisdoms dissolve God's wisdom, in order to render his understanding more and more refined.... It is a time in which man proudly calls himself an adult, only to find that he is a wretched orphan." D. M. M'Intyre (*The Hidden Life of Prayer* [Minneapolis: Dimension, 1969], pp. 22-23) stresses that in prayer we also wrestle against "principalities and powers." From Andrew Bonar he states, "The prince of the power of the air seems to bend all the force of his attack against the spirit of prayer." Modern man struggles against the self. He is pulled on in so many directions that he is distracted from God to self. Only prayer can reunify a man's self which has been so scattered by the enticements of a consumer society. "If prayer is to be genuine, it presupposes an inward battle against the promptings of the world, which denature the relationship with God, and hence denature prayer" (Ellul, *Prayers,* p. 145; cf. pp. 142-46).

JESUS AND PRAYER

In Jesus' day the Jews looked to heaven in both morning and evening, reciting the Shema from Deuteronomy 6:4-5; "Hear, O Israel! The Lord is our God, the Lord is one!" In the afternoon they recited a series of benedictions (an early form of the "Eighteen Benedictions"). In addition they prayed before and after every meal and expressed thanks throughout the day's activities. Finally, there were synagogue services on Monday, Thursday (the market days), and the Sabbath, which included both the Shema and the benedictions as well as the cycle of readings and the sermon. (See Joachim Jeremias, *The Prayers of Jesus* [London: SCM, 1964], pp. 66-72; and Paul F. Bradshaw, *Daily Prayer in the Early Church: A Study of the Origins and Early Development of the Divine Office* [New York: Oxford University Press, 1982], pp. 1-23.) And yet the Jews viewed God as an aloof ruler, who while dwelling among His people in the Holy of Holies, was nonetheless high and lifted up and always far off. Some Jews practiced prayer as an act of obedience to gain merit; others performed it for ostentatious show (Matt. 6:5-8; 23:5).

Jesus transformed the Jewish concept of prayer. First, he prayed at greater length than they. He undoubtedly observed the Jewish prayer times (Mark 6:46; Luke 11:1; 18:1-14) but went further. He prayed for hours and even entire nights (Mark 1:35; 6:46; Luke 6:12). Luke especially stresses how important prayer was for Jesus (3:21; 5:16; 6:12; 9:18). Second, Jesus' model for prayer had a new personal dimension. He prayed using the expression, "Abba, Father." Jews never used the expression in direct address to God, for it was too intimate. Christ, however, made the personal dimension central in the new relationship He established between God and His people. Jeremias writes aptly: "A new way of praying is born. Jesus talks to his Father as naturally, as intimately and with the same sense of security as a child talks to his father. It is a characteristic token of this new mode of prayer that it is dominated by thanksgiving" (*Prayers of Jesus*, p. 78).

THEMES IN PRAYER

Jesus' teaching about prayer had many dimensions. One especially prominent theme was tenacity. Jesus urged tenacity in prayer, as in Matthew 7:7 ("Ask, and it shall be given") and in the parable of the unjust judge of Luke 11. Jeremias calls this "beggar's wisdom." That is, so certain is a person that his request would be received that he refuses to take no for an answer. However, the concept of tenacity in prayer surpasses beggar's wisdom. We continue in prayer because God is faithful and He loves us. He has promised to answer prayer, and He will not fail. Amazingly, Jesus asserted that answers to prayer are certain (Mark 11:22-24). The point was especially stressed in Jesus' farewell discourse of John 14-16, where He gave the absolute promise seven times (14:13, 14; 15:7, 16; 16:23, 24, 26). In that crucial statement there were two emphases: the primary one was that when Jesus departed He would send the Holy Spirit, the Paraclete, to represent Himself; and the secondary theme was that as a result of the Spirit's presence, prayer would be answered. Of course, the promise was not meant to be used selfishly. The key phrase, "in My name," meant that we should be in union with Jesus and His purpose when we pray: "And whatever you ask in My name, that I will do" (John 14:13).[4]

---

4. From *The New King James Version*. Copyright © 1979, 1980, 1982, Thomas Nelson, Inc., Publishers.

Self-centered prayers will not be answered (James 4:3). The power of prayer is kingdom-centered not earth-centered (compare Col. 3:1-4). We earthly parents would hardly give our children what would be bad for them; how much less would the eternal Father, with His perfect knowledge, allow us the harmful thing (Matt. 7:9-11). The sovereignty of God reigns also in the realm of prayer. When God says no to a prayer request, such is an act of love. Therefore, the positive purpose transforms His no to a yes, for it affirms His true will. That is the message of Romans 8:26-27, where Paul admitted, "We do not know how to pray as we should" (literally, "as we must"). The dilemma of finite communication with God is the fact that we cannot see with the eye of God. Yet the security of faith is the certainty that the "Spirit intercedes for us with groanings [which repeat our groanings, v. 23] which surpass human words" and that that intercession is "according to God's will." The promise anchors the truth that the divine refusal to grant a request involves the triune Godhead in a positive demonstration of His will for us.

In Matthew 6:5 (NIV), Jesus stated that if someone prayed in order to gain public approval, his prayer would not be heard, for he would already "have received [his] reward in full." The statement does not mean that prayer meetings are wrong. Believers, however, must be aware of the danger of trying to impress people with their prayers on occasions of public prayer. In similar fashion, Jesus said prayers should be short (Matt. 6:7). The statement most likely referred to public prayers (note the context in Matt. 6), for Jesus Himself often prayed all night. Christ's point is clear: simple, brief prayers are more pleasing to God than ostentatious, lengthy ones.

D. M. M'Intyre states that the necessary equipment for prayer is a quiet place, a quiet hour, and a quiet head (*Hidden Life of Prayer*, pp. 30-38). On occasion, Jesus went by Himself to a mountain, where He could be alone with the Father. For us the exact time of our meeting with the Lord, whether morning, afternoon, or evening, is not especially important. What counts is that we do in fact set aside time to pray.

In the early church believers perceived a distinct connection between prayer and the return of Christ. Bradshaw asserts in *Daily Prayer* (pp. 37-39) that Christians took quite literally Jesus' injunction in the Garden of Gethsemane, "Watch and pray that ye may not enter temptation" (Matt. 26:41, KJV). The concept of watchfulness is repeated often in the epistles (Col. 4:2; Eph. 6:18; cf. Phil. 4:5-6; 1 Pet. 4:7). It is specifically seen in the Lord's Prayer (Matt. 6:9-13), with its progression from "Hallowed by Thy name" to "Thy kingdom come" to "Thy will be done," a progression also reflected in the Jewish Kaddish prayer that concludes the synagogue service. Prayer was one of the primary means by which the early Christians kept themselves in a state of readiness for the Lord's return. We should engage in prayer for the same reason. Do we not communicate through letters with a loved one who has been gone a long time so that we are ready to see him when he returns? May we not communicate through prayer with our returning Lord?

Finally, we find in Christ's teachings and in the experiences of the New Testament Christians an emphasis upon corporate prayer. The New Testament simply has no concept of Christians' growing in the Lord in isolation from one another. The same is true of prayer. The early church probably continued Jesus' practice of observing the three daily prayer times of the Jews. In Luke 24:53 and Acts 1:14 the disciples continued in daily corporate prayer (both in the Temple and among themselves) between the ascension and Pentecost. In Acts 2:42, "prayers"[5] certainly refers to the fixed corporate prayers of the church as one of the pillars of its fellowship (see also Acts 4:24; 5:12). The early church did not consider public prayer an option but a vital necessity. The church could not maintain its unity or spiritual vitality without hands uplifted in prayer (1 Tim. 2:8, NIV; "I want men everywhere to lift up holy hands in prayer, without anger or disputing"). In the second century, Didache 8:3 mentions three prayer times as well; it is likely that the observance continued into the later church. Corporate prayer is needed no less today. Prayer provides the holy lubricant that allows the church to more forward without friction.

POWER IN PRAYER

Some consider prayer almost a magical formula. In our consumer society, it is common to think of prayer as containing the power to get things from God. The average person equates prayer with intercession and thinks little of its true purpose. Primarily, prayer must change us. Prayer is not intended to change the mind of God, as if He needs to be convinced to help us or somehow lacks the power to work unless we ask Him. We pray in order to align ourselves with Him, to commune with Him. The first order of prayer is to seek the mind of God, not just in terms of His will but more in terms of His priorities, His outlook. Prayer is communion, then communication. The great men of God, the prayer warriors, sought to know God's mind before they asked His

---

5. From *The New King James Version.* Copyright © 1979, 1980, 1982, Thomas Nelson, Inc., Publishers.

intervention in their affairs. This is prayer's foremost power. As E. M. Bounds has written, "Prayer freshens the heart of the preacher, keeps it in tune with God and in sympathy with the people, lifts his ministry out of the chilly air of a profession, fructifies routine and moves every wheel with the facility and power of a divine intervention" (*Power Through Prayer* [London: Marshall, Morgan and Scott, n.d.], p. 30). Bounds adds (pp. 32-33): "No learning can make up for the failure to pray. No earnestness, no diligence, no study, no gifts will supply its lack. Talking to men for God is a great thing, but talking to God for men is greater still. He will never talk well and with great success to men for God who has not learned well how to talk to God for men."

Prayer is a channel, a funnel through which the presence of God flows. Prayer does change things, but not as if God is normally absent from the believer's situation. Rather, prayer brings about an increase in His presence, such that there are "streams of living water" flowing out (John 7:38, NIV) from the person praying. In John the "living water" is the Holy Spirit, and it is His presence that brings about change. The passage also intimates why the prayers of many are more efficacious than the supplication of one. They channel even more of the power of the Spirit into the needed area.

THE METHODOLOGY OF PRAYER

There is no better illustration of the difficulty of disciplined prayer than the famous prayer of Thomas Merton. It is quoted here as it appeared in Gregory A. Youngchild's paper, "Seasons of Prayer," *Theological Students' Fellowship Bulletin* 4, no. 1 (November 1980): 10:

> I have no idea where I am going. I do not see the road ahead of me. I cannot know for certain where it will end. Nor do I really know myself, and the fact that I think I am following your will does not mean that I am actually doing so. But I believe that the desire to please you does in fact please you. And I hope I have that desire in all that I am doing. I hope that I will never do anything apart from that desire. And I know that if I do this you will lead me by the right road, though I may know nothing about it. Therefore I will trust you always though I may seem to be lost and in the shadow of death. I will not fear, for you are ever with me, and you will never leave me to face my perils alone.

Some of us can readily identify with Merton's prayer.

Richard J. Foster, in *Celebration of Discipline* ([New York: Harper & Row, 1978], pp. 32-40), discusses the *how* of prayer. First, he points out that deep prayer does not come of itself but must be learned. We should study biblical teachings on prayer to see the God-given patterns. For instance, New Testament prayers were positive rather than tentative; those who made them expected things to happen. As William Carey said, "Attempt great things for God, expect great things from God." In addition, we should study the past masters to learn their secrets. Next, we should learn from mistakes and keep careful watch on our prayer lives to see what works best. We should learn to listen to God, to meditate upon Him when preparing the heart for prayer. Often the Spirit will commune with us and lead us into the proper prayer. The simple faith of a child can help us imagine the needs of the prayer and fulfill Hebrews 11:1, "Faith is the substance of things hoped for, the evidence of things not seen" (KJV). Finally, we must be willing to take the time necessary for such strenuous effort.

I would suggest a prayer notebook and a disciplined use of it. One of the daunting things in prayer is the number of needs. A notebook can solve the issue. Put down the needs of which you are aware and then pray through only a portion of your list each day if it is too long. Divide the list up into personal needs, family needs, friends, church, missions, and a miscellaneous category for other requests. Also, leave a column for answers, and add notes explaining how the prayer was answered (for the sake of the future). You could prepare personal and family notebooks. Keeping such notebooks will not only aid the quality of your prayer life but will protect you from one of the most common of all broken promises, "I will be praying for you."

Finally, learn to pray Scripture. In so doing you will combine meditation with prayer. The Psalms come first to mind, but the intercessory prayers of Paul or the great prayers of the Old Testament saints (e.g., Dan. 9:3–19) can be tremendous aids to vital prayer. After choosing the passage, you may want to study it inductively and write down the various injuctions in your own words as prayer requests for yourself.

CONCLUSION

Presence of mind is a difficult thing to maintain in modern America. This essay proposes that the pressures of the world upon us can be alleviated when we maintain the presence of God in the mind. Bible study and prayer are two means to bring about that end. Indeed, this is one occasion when we can truthfully say the end justifies the means. If we spend hours each week filling our minds with secular concepts by way of television, the newspaper, magazines, and novels, how much more should we take time to fill our minds with the truths of our Lord. Christ set the pattern for us with His emphasis on prayer. If the very

Son of God needed constant communion with the Father, how much more we?

Many Christians labor under a somewhat mistaken view of the devotional life. They make an unfortunate dichotomy between seeking truth and enriching their lives, as if seeking truth did not enrich their life. The result is that those oriented toward the former are information-gatherers, often without a concern for a practical Christian lifestyle. Their writings and sermons rarely change lives or make the Bible seem relevant. Those oriented toward the practical side of things, on the other hand, sometimes manipulate the biblical texts and emphasize an unharnessed emotional Christianity. We are trying to establish a method here that involves the mind as well as the volition and emotions. We are proposing that Christians should be whole persons who seek to live out the revealed truths of Scripture, to apply the Word of God to the needs of their neighbors.

Bible study provides the concepts, and prayer the communion. They are two aspects of communication with God. Our minds must be steeped in the Lord Jesus Christ. Paul recognized this in his marvelous prayer of Ephesians 3:17-19 (NIV),

> And I pray that you, being rooted and established in love, may have power, together with all the saints, to grasp how wide and long and high and deep is the love of Christ, and to know this love that surpasses knowledge—that you may be filled to the measure of all the fullness of God.

Note what constitutes being "filled" with the "fullness of God": the comprehension and knowledge (both acts of the mind) of the divine love. The devotional life is not only a mystic experience, but it includes rational thinking at the deepest level, as the believer seeks to have the mind of Christ. This Holy Spirit-given mind-set, and it alone, can counteract the secular onslaught against renewing our minds as faithful Christians.

7 The Christian Life as Battleground: Pastor Martin Luther's Counsel

John D. Woodbridge

Martin, how can you assume that you are the only one to understand the sense of Scripture? Would you put your judgment above that of so many famous men and claim that you know more than they all?

Johann Eck's challenge to Luther at Worms, April 1521

Unless I am convinced by Scripture, and plain reason, I do not accept the authority of popes and councils, for they have contradicted each other. . . . My conscience is captive to the Word of God; I cannot and will not recant anything, for to go against conscience is neither right nor safe. God help me, Amen.

Luther's defense at Worms, April 1521

On the screen of our imaginations, the Protestant Reformer Martin Luther often casts an image bigger than life. We find it difficult to believe that this stalwart individual, who stood alone against the ecclesiastical establishment of his day, was a flesh and blood person subject to the same self doubts and temptations that we have. We tend to forget that, unlike Christ, Luther sinned, suffered pangs of depression and guilt for his sin, and wrestled in more than a few losing bouts with the devil. Perhaps it is because we view Luther from the distance of more than four hundred years and because we know so much about his wide-ranging influence that he takes on Titan dimensions for us. It is true that Luther *was* singularly used of God in launching the

Protestant Reformation. His recovery of the doctrine of justification by faith alone and his insistence upon the authority of the Scriptures alone *have* helped scores of people to understand better how to know God. Because of those very accomplishments, however, many of us have tended to lift the German reformer out of the ranks of mere mortals.

This loss of Luther's humanity is unfortunate. We can better identify with his insights concerning knowing God if we remember that Luther, too, was shaped out of human clay. He faced many of the same daily struggles we experience. He won some spiritual battles; he lost others. On some occasions the rough-hewn Saxon was happy and as carefree as a lark. He enjoyed singing praises to his God. On other occasions he was deeply depressed; he blasphemed God and believed that the Holy One had deserted him. Luther described a severe depression which overtook him in 1527 with these words: "I was shaken by desperation and blasphemy of God" (Roland Bainton, *Here I Stand: A Life of Martin Luther* [New York: New American Library, 1950], p. 283; hereafter, Bainton, *Life*).

Luther's life (1483–1546) and thought are truly remarkable, and they have attracted the attention of an army of scholars. More books have been written about Luther than nearly any other man or woman of history. It is not our purpose to survey Luther's life here. Roland Bainton's captivating biography of Luther (see above) should more than satisfy the reader interested in Luther's reforming and church building activities. Nor is it our purpose to review the complexity of Luther's thought or to resolve its ambiguities. A book such as Paul Althaus's *The Theology of Martin Luther* (Philadelphia: Fortress, 1966; hereafter, Althaus, *Theology*) would be useful in that task. What concerns us more is the man Luther, who possessed a warm pastor's heart. We want to learn about this Luther who sought through the writing of catechisms, commentaries, and personal letters, and through the spoken word to help his immediate family and followers walk with God. Luther himself knew God well; his counsel is most valuable for us.

Because Luther saw theology and lived Christian experience as inseparably united, we will discuss some of his formal theological concepts. But our emphasis will be upon Luther's practical sugges-tions to his fellow Christians concerning the devotional life. We will cite his own words at some length. In having Luther speak for himself, we can better appreciate the strength of his convictions and the deep compassion of his heart. As we shall see, Martin Luther's own model-ing and instruction in the devotional life are as helpful for us today as they were for Christians more than four hundred years ago. Knowing God was one of Luther's chief occupations.

THE NEW BIRTH: AN ALL-IMPORTANT SPIRITUAL BEGINNING

According to his own testimony, Luther's attitudes about God changed dramatically when he experienced a spiritual new birth (see Christ's discussion of the new birth in John 3). Like many of his contemporaries in the early sixteenth century, Luther was troubled by the wrenching question of his personal salvation. How could he please God? He entered a monastery where he struggled to pursue a life of good works and self-denial. Would not perfect obedience to harsh monastic regulations placate God? Frustration met him at every turn. He discovered to his dismay that not only was he incapable of living a sin-free life, but that his own sinfulness polluted even his motivations for doing good. His gnawing sense of guilt did not desert him even when he followed monastic discipline in a scrupulous fashion. As to God, Luther hated Him. In a famous account of his quest for personal salvation, Luther described his predicament as a monk:

> My situation was that, although an impeccable monk, I stood before God as a sinner troubled in conscience, and I had no confidence that my merit would assuage him. Therefore I did not love a just and angry God, but rather hated and murmured against him.
>
> (Bainton, *Life,* p. 49)

In this perilous state Luther, a keen Bible student (he served as a doctor of sacred Scripture), clung to the apostle Paul, hoping against hope to discover some biblical way out from his unsettling dilemma.

After careful Bible study, Luther began to understand the meaning of Psalm 31:1*b*, Romans 3:28, and Paul's teaching on justification by faith alone. Thereafter, and to his great joy, he experienced a spiritual new birth:

> Night and day I pondered until I saw the connection between the justice of God and the statement that "the just shall live by his faith." Then I grasped that the justice of God is that righteousness by which through grace and sheer mercy God justifies us through faith. Thereupon I felt myself to be reborn and to have gone through open doors into paradise.
>
> (Bainton, *Life,* p. 49)

Luther was now attuned to the heartbeat of Pauline theology: we are justified by God, not because of our works, but because of our faith in Christ. Even our faith is a work of God within us. Luther now understood that salvation is indeed a free gift of God's grace; it is not a prize earned by our tireless though vain efforts to persuade Him that we are "good enough."

Luther's new awareness of God's gracious provision for man's salvation in Christ led him quite naturally to revise his former estimation that God was a tyrant. In the account of his "conversion" (set in quotation marks because Luther used the expression "breakthrough" to describe his new birth experience and because Luther frequently identified the new birth with water baptism),[1] Luther continued:

> If you have a true faith that Christ is your Savior, then at once you have a gracious God, for faith leads you in and opens God's heart and will, that you should see pure grace and overflowing love. This it is to behold God in faith that you should look upon his fatherly, friendly heart, in which there is no anger nor ungraciousness. He who sees God as angry does not see him rightly but looks only on a curtain, as if a dark cloud had been drawn across his face.
>
> (Bainton, *Life,* p. 50)

For Luther, a person begins to gain some knowledge of God as He really is after that individual is born again into God's spiritual family. Luther knew this to be true from his own experience. Before his "conversion," he hated God, the tyrant; after it, he began to love God, the caring Father.

Luther felt deeply pained that some of his fellow Europeans did not understand the new birth. There was a simple though literally damning reason for their lack of comprehension: they had never experienced true Christian faith. They wore lightly a cultural Christianity. Tragically, biblical Christianity was foreign to them. In his treatise *On Christian Liberty* Luther commented on their plight:

> Christian faith has appeared to many an easy matter; of whom not a few have classed it among the moral virtues, nay, have made it merely a sort of attendant on virtue. And this they have done because they have never proved what it is in their own experience, nor internally tasted its power. Whereas no one can truly describe it himself, nor really understand it when truly described, unless he has at some time, under the fiery trial of pressing conflicts, tasted the spirit of it in his own soul. And he who has

1. For a discussion of the new birth as it relates to baptism in Luther's thought, see Herman A. Preus, *A Theology to Live by: The Practical Luther for the Practicing Christian* (St. Louis: Concordia, 1977), pp. 151-56; hereafter, Preus, *Theology.* For many years Luther struggled to clarify in his own teaching the relationship between justification by faith alone and baptismal regeneration. During severe temptations Luther referred back to his baptism ("I have been baptized") as he attempted to fend off the devil.

really tasted this, even in the smallest degree, can never write of it, speak
of it, think of it, nor hear of it enough; for it is, as Christ calls it, "a living
fountain springing up into everlasting life." (John 4)[2]

Luther tells us that only if we have experienced the new birth (that is,
have been born into God's spiritual family) do we begin to know that
God is a gracious father rather than an angry bully. Only if we have
passed through the new birth do we begin, with the psalmist, to
partake of salvation's authentic joys.

These teachings of Luther about knowing God are important. We
would do well to consider them in detail.

THE GOD WHO IS REALLY THERE

After his "conversion," Luther's awe of God did not diminish. True it
is that God is our Heavenly Father, but He is also the Almighty One
who rules the world. Luther did not shrink back from the full implications of 1 Corinthians 12:6: "God . . . works all in all" (NKJV). The
verse meant for him that God causes the darkening skies to be suddenly transfixed by jagged bolts of lightening; He causes the heavens to
resound with the clap of thunder. It meant that God is the master of
human history. It meant that God will have His way. As hard as it is for
us to believe this, nations do rise and plummet at His good pleasure.
Though intellectuals or just plain people curse God or deny His existence,
they cannot escape His presence or His judgment. Wrote Luther: "He
is present everywhere, even in death, in hell, among his enemies, yes,
even in their hearts. For he has made and rules everything so that it
must do his will" (Althaus, *Theology*, p. 111). He is, in Francis
Schaeffer's terms, the God who is there. All is in God's hands.

With such an awe-struck impression of God, Luther was not prone
to speculate about the mysteries of the *Deus nudus* (the naked God),
including the inner workings of the Godhead and God's hidden will.
There were the forbidden realms into which the rationalistic schoolmen
(called scholastics) had so unflinchingly and yet so disasterously tried
to probe.[3] There were the realms in which some of the mystics had

---

2. Cited in E. Y. Mullins, *Why Is Christianity True?* (Chicago: Christian
   Culture Press, 1950), p. 242. See also Theodore Tappert, ed., *Luther:
   Letters of Spiritual Counsel* (Philadelphia: Westeminster, 1955), p. 110;
   hereafter, Tappert, *Letters*.
3. Luther blamed Aristotle's influence for this tendency among Christian
   scholastics. He denounced Aristotle as "this accursed, proud, knavish
   heathen" who had introduced terms and concepts into Christian theology
   that could not easily be reconciled with biblical revelation.

touted special exercises for entering into union with God. Luther did not disparage the right use of regenerated reason in theology. Nor did he deny the validity of much teaching by Christian mystics, especially that of Johann Tauler.[4] He believed, however, that any man-made attempt at capturing God's essence through rational speculation or through mystical merging with the Almighty were doomed to failure. Moreover, he thought it was presumptuous for us creatures to try brazenly to plunge the depths of the Creator's Being and hidden will. Concerning God's will, Luther noted that it "is not to be curiously inquired into, but to be adored with reverence as the most profound secret of His divine majesty" (cited in Skevington Wood, *Captive to the Word: Martin Luther, Doctor of Sacred Scripture* [Devon, England: Paternoster, 1969], p. 131). Luther reverentially wanted to leave certain mysterious subjects as they were, off limits.

GENERAL KNOWLEDGE OF GOD AND PARTICULAR KNOWLEDGE OF GOD

Before his "conversion" Luther had known something about God as the all-powerful ruler of the universe. Afterward, he would argue that all unbelievers have a general knowledge of God but that they lack a particular knowledge of Him. Luther reflected on this matter in commenting on Galatians 4:8:

> If all men knew God, wherefore doth Paul say, that the Galatians knew not God before the preaching of the Gospel? I answer, there is a double knowledge of God, general and particular. All men have the general knowledge, namely, that there is a God, that He created heaven and earth, that He is just, that He punisheth the wicked. But what God thinketh of us, what His will is toward us, what He will give or what He will do to the end we may be delivered from sin and death, and be saved (which is the true knowledge of God indeed), this they know not. As it may be that I know some man by sight, whom indeed I know not thoroughly, because I understand not what affection he beareth towards me.[5]

4. On the complex relationships that exist between Luther's thought and Christian mysticism, see Bengt R. Hoffman, *Luther and the Mystics: A Re-Examination of Luther's Spiritual Experience and His Relationship to the Mystics* (Minneapolis: Augsburg, 1976); hereafter, Hoffman, *Luther and the Mystics.* Luther complained that certain mystics sometimes advocated the abandonment of rationality in the quest to know God: "This is what mystical theology declares: Abandon your intellect and senses and rise up above being and non-being" (*Luther's Works: Table Talk,* vol. 54, p. 112; hereafter, Luther, *Table Talk*).
5. Cited in Philip S. Watson, *Let God Be God! An Interpretation of the Theology of Martin Luther* (London: Epworth, 1960), p. 73.

Although God has afforded unbelievers with this general knowledge of Himself, they inevitably distort it and create a god of their own imagination (Rom. 1-2). They fall into idolatry because they manufacture and worship a god or gods who do not exist rather than the true God who is really there.

Sometimes the god they create is a relatively tame one. Such a god can be pacified by good works, including mortifications of the flesh and the observance of certain religious rituals or by the purchase of indulgences. According to Luther, many church people of his own day were sadly attempting to please this god.

Sometimes he is an uncontrollable tyrant, like the one Luther had conjured up before his conversion. During a lightning storm a terrified Luther had prayed in the name of St. Anne that this god might spare his life. Luther survived the storm. Thereafter he entered the monastery, believing in a god who resembled more a fearsome Vulcan of the skies than the Lord Jehovah. (Some historians have suggested that the "god" whom Luther feared when he entered the monstery had some of the attributes of the young man's stern father.) This god was whimsical. He struck down arbitarily the innocent and guilty alike through accidents, plagues, wars, and famines.

Whereas his awe of this latter god had led Luther to fear and hatred, once he was born again, the Reformer's awe of the true Almighty God moved him to trust. He grasped one of the most incredible and joyful messages from heaven that a Christian learns: the Almighty God is one in the same with our heavenly Father. Luther could commit his life and those of his family and friends to such a God. This he did, and in full confidence and love.

The Lord's Prayer became a treasure trove for him. Not only did he study it carefully in order to unpack fully its meaning, but, as we shall see, he prayed it daily in his devotions: "Our Father who art in Heaven . . . " In addition, he boldly uttered the phrase of the prayer that stops the heart of a secular humanist who glories in his much-vaunted autonomy: "Thy will be done on earth as it is in heaven."

In sum, Luther tells us that our general knowledge of God's existence and power must be supplemented by a particular knowledge of His goodness and graciousness: "God is truly known not when we are aware of his power or his wisdom, which are terrible, but only when we know his goodness and his love" (Althaus, *Theology,* p. 191).

GOD'S REVELATIONS TO MANKIND: THE LIVING WORD, CHRIST, AND THE WRITTEN WORD, THE SCRIPTURES

If the created order and our conscience act as masks to reveal God only in His terrible power, wisdom, and righteousness, how do men and women learn to know God as gracious and good? From what other sources comes this all-important particular knowledge of God? Luther proposes that God has taken the initiative to reveal this saving knowledge to us. He has done so in the incarnate living Word, Christ, and in the written Word of God, the Scriptures.

THE LIVING WORD, CHRIST

Jesus Christ is God in the flesh. He is, as Luther said so well, "the mirror of God's fatherly heart." Did not Christ declare that "he who has seen me has seen the Father" (John 14:9)? In 1519 Luther wrote a friend: "Whoever wishes to think about or to meditate on God in a way that will lead him to salvation must subordinate everything else to the humanity of Christ" (Althaus, *Theology,* p. 183). In Christ, the Son of God, the Father is revealed as compassionate and loving.

In sending Christ to earth, the Father demonstrated his concern for man's redemption. The God who rolls the thunder and splashes lightening through the gathering dark skies is the same God as the one who, because He loved the world so much, "gave his only begotten son" (John 3:16, KJV) to die on a cross. Commenting on Philippians 2:5ff, Luther noted the pleasure God takes in what Christ has done for us:

> Thus Paul opens the heavens with one word and clears the way for us to look into the depths of the divine majesty and see the gracious will and love of his fatherly heart for us, which cannot be expressed in words. Paul wants us to feel that God has from all eternity been pleased with what that glorious person Christ should do and has done for us. Whose heart does not simply melt for joy at hearing this?
>
> (Althaus, *Theology,* pp. 187–88)

In a word, we learn of God's wonderful goodness and grace through meditating upon Christ, the Incarnate Word of God.

How has God provided for our salvation in Christ? How can we sinners who "cannot will anything but what he [Satan] wills" (Luther) be saved from Satan's kingdom? Through His death on the cross and resurrection from the grave, Christ vanquished our great foes, sin and death. Moreover, He defeated Satan, that treacherous enemy of our souls. The sinless One took our place at Calvary and made possible our salvation. Indeed, Luther emphasized the Incarnation as the full identification by God-in-Christ with humanity. By faith we can say to Christ: "My sin lies on you and your innocence and righteousness now belong to me." In that we then become clothed in Christ's righteousness, God no longer sees us wearing the tattered rags of our sin. He can declare us righteous, even though we remain sinners (or rather sinner-saints). We have been "justified by faith." Nor can we claim that we did anything to bring about our own salvation. We did not choose God; He chose us. Even our faith in Christ finds its origins in God's grace, for God implants it within us: "True faith cannot be manufactured by our own thoughts, for it is solely a work of God in us, without any assistance on our part" (Preus, *Theology,* p. 99). God's provision for His chosen ones, then, is total. It is an evidence of His unfathomable love for His children as a heavenly Father.

Only a person who understands that his salvation depends completely upon God's grace begins to grasp how much he should worship, praise, and serve Him with thankful heart. Luther believed that one reason individuals failed to do those things was that they attributed much of their experience to their own initiative. Luther saw life otherwise: "Whoever understands this [that God works all in all] soon becomes aware that he cannot make the smallest movement or even think unless God causes it: that his life is not completely in his own hand but solely and completely in God's hand" (Althaus, *Theology,* p. 112, n. 27). Sharp was the contrast between the God-centered focus of Luther's religion and the man-centered orientation of many churchmen of his day.

What kind of faith is it by which we are justified? Luther pointed out that it is not to be equated with belief about God: "Firstly, our belief may be *about* God, as is the case when I accept what is said about Him, in the same way as I accept what is said about the Turks, or the devil, or hell" (cited in Bertram Woolf, ed., *Reformation Writings of Martin Luther* [New York: Philosophical Library, 1953], 1:83; hereafter Woolf, *Reformation Writings*). For Luther, that kind of believing was not true faith. Rather it was a kind of knowledge. On the contrary, Luther identified saving faith with belief *in* God:

> This is the case where I do not merely accept what is said about God, but I put my faith in Him, I surrender myself to Him; I venture to enter into association with Him, believing without any hesitation that He will be to me, and act towards me, just as we are taught He will.
>
> (Woolf, *Reformation Writings,* 1:83)

Or he described what saving faith involves in these terms:

> The kind of faith which dares to accept what is said of God, even if doing so means risking life or death, is the faith which alone makes a man a Christian; through it all his desires are satisfied by God. This kind of faith is unknown to those who are evil and sinful at heart, for it is a living faith.
>
> (Woolf, *Reformation Writings*, 1:83-84)

Such a faith goes beyond a knowledge about God to an utter confidence in Him.

In some ways saving faith allows us to become one with God. This is not the union of our beings with God's being that the mystics envisioned. It is a union of wills; we begin to want to do God's will.[6] It is a union of minds; we begin to perceive spiritual realities as God sees them. We are God's children; we are new creations in Christ. The Holy Spirit works for our sanctification.

Luther described the believer's close association with Christ in this fashion: "But faith must be taught correctly, namely, that by it you are so cemented to Christ that He and you are as one person, which cannot be separated but remains attached to Him forever" (Hoffman, *Luther and the Mystics*, p. 174). Elsewhere the Reformer noted: "Faith not only gives the soul enough for her to become, like the divine word, gracious, free, and blessed. It also unites the soul with Christ, like a bride with the bridegroom, and, from this marriage, Christ and the Soul become one body, as St. Paul says" (Woolf, *Reformation Writings*, 1: 363).

Luther spoke about a saving faith he had experienced. Once he had understood Paul's teaching about justification by faith alone, he did not hold back. With full confidence he threw himself into the arms of the loving heavenly Father who had sent Christ into the world. God could be trusted with his life. Such was the faith that fortified poor struggling Brother Martin. It made him willing to risk body and earthly treasure in order to preach the good news of salvation to all, whether they be Renaissance popes or rustic peasants.

THE WRITTEN WORD, THE SCRIPTURES

For Luther, God chose to reveal Himself not only in Christ, the living Word of God, but also in the Holy Scriptures, the written Word of

6. Karl Holl, *What Did Luther Understand by Religion?* ed. James L. Adams and Walter F. Bense; trans. Fred W. Meuser and Walter R. Wietzke (Philadelphia: Fortress, 1977), pp. 83-84; hereafter, Holl, *Religion*.

God. In that Christ is the focal point of the entire Scriptures, Luther viewed the two Words as inseparably related to each other. In the Scriptures God reveals Himself through the words which its human authors penned as they were inspired by the Holy Spirit. The resultant Scriptures, according to Luther, were the inerrant Word of God and His supreme written authority:

> But everyone, indeed, knows that at times they [the fathers] have erred as men will; therefore, I am ready to trust them only when they prove their opinions from Scripture, which has never erred.[7]

In the Scriptures we find truth about God, salvation, and the world. Luther put it this way: "Ah, who knows how far that is true which is set forth in the Scriptures?"[8]

The Holy Spirit who inspired the writing of the Scriptures takes the words of Scripture and brings their spiritual import home to us: "Faith comes only through the work of the Holy Spirit and that is done only through the external word" (Althaus, *Theology*, pp. 36–37). Our knowledge of God as gracious and good comes, then, through either our hearing the Word of God, as through preaching, for example, or through our reading of that same Word. (Luther also joined the sacraments very closely to preaching as the "words" of God.) The Holy Spirit does not speak through new revelations but is bound to the Scriptures alone. Since God has chosen to communicate to us through His written Word, we stay away from the Scriptures at our great peril. The distinguished Luther scholar Paul Althaus summarized well Luther's position on this key point:

> God's word in the hand of his Spirit is simply indispensable for man's soul and spirit. The soul is created for the word, and it cannot live without the word of God. It can get along without everything else but not without the word.
>
> (Althaus, *Theology*, p. 41)

In any meaningful devotional life Christians must give special attention to the Scriptures.

How should we study God's written Word? We should seek its

---

7. Althaus, *Theology*, p. 6, n. 12. For Luther's adherence to biblical authority and inerrancy, see M. Reu, "Luther and the Scriptures," *The Springfielder*, August 1960, pp. 9–111.
8. Thomas S. Kepler, ed., *The Table Talk of Martin Luther* (Grand Rapids: Baker, 1952), p. 10; hereafter, Kepler, *Table Talk*.

meaning through prayer and meditation. We should not engage in rational speculation about it. Luther wrote: "We ought not to criticize, explain, or judge the Scriptures by our mere reason, but diligently, with prayer, meditate thereon, and seek their meaning" (Kepler, *Table Talk*, p. 6). In the *Preface to German Writings* (1539), Luther summarized his approach to Bible study. First, preparatory prayer (*oratio*):

> Kneel down in your little room [Matt. 6:6] and pray to God with real humility and earnestness, that he through his dear Son may give you his Holy Spirit, who will enlighten you, lead you, and give you understanding.

Second, meditation (*meditatio*):

> You should meditate, that is, not only in your heart, but also externally, by actually repeating and comparing oral speech and literal words of the book, reading and rereading them with diligent attention and reflection, so that you may see what the Holy Spirit means by them.

Third, testing that comes after studying God's Word (*tentatio*):

> For as soon as God's Word takes root and grows in you, the devil will harry you, and will make a real doctor of you, and by his assaults will teach you to seek and love God's Word.[9]

Whether an individual is a layperson or a theologian, he or she should study the Bible in this way and expect to be tempted afterwards.

It is interesting to notice that Luther believed that God, the Holy Spirit, speaks to us through the written Word more obviously on some occasions than on others. Because we never know when God may communicate with us in a special way through His Word, the Reformer suggested that we should take every opportunity to come into contact with the Word of God. In addition, Luther believed that our hearing the preached Word and our participation in the Lord's Supper (in which Christ is also present) are highly important for our spiritual communion with the Lord. That a Christian could live in isolation from the church was nearly unthinkable for Luther. Luther proposed that God could communicate with the believer even during the ser-

---

9. *Luther's Works: Career of the Reformer IV,* vol 34., ed. Lewis W. Spitz and Helmut T. Lehmann (Philadelphia: Fortress, 1960), pp. 285–87. Luther made these comments when discussing "a correct way of studying theology."

mons of inept preachers. Thus, though we may suspect that the sermon will be boring, we should not risk missing a church service.

> Since the preachers have the office, the name, and the honor of being God's co-workers, no one should think that he is so learned or so holy that he may despise or miss the most insignificant sermon. This is especially true because he does not know at what time the hour will come in which God will do His work in him through the preachers.
>
> (Althaus, *Theology,* p. 40)

Furthermore, during our private reading of the Scriptures, we should pause time and again to listen for any particular communication the Lord might have for us from the Scriptures. That is, we should literally wait upon God to speak to us through His Word. Devotional activities that are rushed or carried out in a mindless way lose most of their value; but those Christians who wait upon the Lord "shall renew their strength" (Isa. 40:31, KJV).

Our knowledge of God, therefore, is not dependent upon our own faculties for rational speculation, nor upon our efforts to induce a mystical experience through following spiritual exercises of one sort or another. Rather God has graciously taken the initiative to disclose Himself to us through Christ the living Word, and through the Scriptures, the written Word. And today God still takes the initiative to speak to us through His Word, the Scriptures, whose principal subject is Christ, the incarnated Word. And yet our knowledge of God remains partial. Our spiritual sensitivities as Christians remain impaired by sin so that we see "through a glass darkly." Our understanding of God is childlike. But what knowledge we do have of God only causes us to marvel at the mystery of His goodness and love towards us as evidenced in Christ, the Incarnated Word, and in the Scriptures, the Written Word.

THE CHRISTIAN LIFE: A BATTLEGROUND

According to Luther, the Christian life has moments of true joy and peace. But it is also characterized by moments of depression and by hand-to-hand combat with the devil. The Christian's life can be justly described as a battleground between God and Satan and between the spirit and the flesh. Luther realized that Satan is not at all pleased when potential candidates for hell become God's children through the new birth. The son of perdition, that wifely and perverse one, does not rest on his devilish oars. Although his ultimate defeat has already been achieved at the cross, he continues to hound Christians. Wrote Luther,

"In brief, the devil is determined to blast God's love from a man's mind and to arouse thoughts of God's wrath."[10] He seeks to reassert control over men's wills and to disrupt their communion with the caretaker of their souls, their heavenly Father. He constantly tries to keep them far removed from Jesus Christ, the living Word; from the Scriptures, the written Word; and from the sacraments. Sometimes his deceptions are subtle; Christians become weak and lose their evangelical warmth without perceiving their worsening state. Sometimes his deceptions are blatant; Christians plunge headlong into gross sin. But in either case Christians are tricked: the sweet-smelling bread that Satan offers always turns out to be hard stone.

More than most of us, Luther understood the impact of Satan's power upon Christians' daily living. He struggled frequently with Satan and with demons. The story goes that he once threw an inkbottle at the devil who had appeared in his room. Sometimes Luther lost those battles, found himself overwhelmed by despair, and believed that God was far removed from him. In this regard Luther was like many of us. With an awareness of his own weaknesses and with firsthand knowledge of the devil's clever devices, Luther devoted much of his time in advising fellow Christians how they might persevere in the Christian life, how they might fend off Satan, whom Luther called "a strong man armed."

For Luther all of life was to be lived in faith. Even the most humble act, such as collecting straw, if performed in faith, was more pleasing to God than a widely acclaimed act performed without it. Luther went so far as to declare that, without faith, it is not a good work even to raise all the dead or to give one's body to be burned.[11] All moments of life were to be devoted to God in faith. Nonetheless, there were times of day Luther set aside for what we would call devotions, that is, periods of prayer and Bible reading.

DEVOTIONS: THE IMPORTANCE OF THE TEN COMMANDMENTS, THE APOSTLES' CREED, AND THE LORD'S PRAYER

Martin Luther advocated a devotional program that he himself practiced and found most helpful. In the twilight years of his life, Luther reportedly indicated that his own devotions centered in meditation

10. *Luther's Works: Devotional Writings I,* vol. 42, ed. Martin O. Dietrich and Helmut T. Lehmann (Philadelphia: Fortress, 1969), p. 103; hereafter, *Writings I.*
11. Martin Luther, "A Treatise on Good Works, 1520," *Works of Martin Luther: With Introduction and Notes,* The Philadelphia Edition (reprint; Grand Rapids: Baker, 1982), 1:189.

upon the Ten Commandments, the Apostles' Creed, and the Lord's Prayer:

> Though I am an old doctor of divinity, to this day I have not got beyond the children's learning—the Ten Commandments, the Belief, and the Lord's Prayer; and these I understand not so well as I should, though I study them daily, praying with my son John and my daughter Magdelen.
>
> (Kepler, *Table Talk*, p. 9)

This statement, found in Luther's *Table Talk*, appears to be authentic. The devotional program it contains is the same one Luther had recommended to fellow Christians much earlier in his career. In 1520, Luther published *A Short Exposition of the Decalogue, the Apostles' Creed and the Lord's Prayer*, a piece that pulsates with the Reformer's own spiritual vitality. In it, Luther outlined what he believed was a God-ordained perspective on the devotional life:

> Surely it has been specially ordained by God that the people in general, who cannot read the Scriptures for themselves, should learn, and know by heart, the Ten Commandments, the Apostles' Creed, and the Lord's Prayer. They contain the whole substance of the Scriptures, and should be expounded time and again. They also contain everything that a Christian needs to know; they put the essentials in summary form; and also they are quickly and easily grasped.
>
> (Woolf, *Reformation Writings*, 1:71)

Luther believed that Christians who were non-readers (the vast majority of Europeans in his day could not read) should memorize these compact statements and use them as the basis for spiritual reflection. As time went on, Luther became more adamant about this. He had discovered among villagers an appalling ignorance of the rudiments of Christianity: "Though all are called Christians and partake of the Holy Sacrament, they know neither the Lord's Prayer, nor the Creed, nor the Ten Commandments, but live like the poor cattle and senseless swine" (Henry Bettenson, ed., *Documents of the Christian Church*, 2d ed. [New York: Oxford University Press, 1970], p. 202). Luther urged that those who would not memorize those statements should not be admitted to the Sacrament; they were "no Christians." Luther even threatened that they should be handed over to the devil. In 1529 Luther created two catechisms, the *Large Catechism for Adults* and the *Small Catechism for Children* to help ordinary people learn the basics of Christianity. Both catechisms were structured around the Ten Commandments, the Apostles' Creed, and the Lord's Prayer.

As for those Christians who could read, Luther believed they should memorize the statements also. To help readers understand what they had memorized, Luther, with a pastor's deep concern, commented on each element of the Decalogue, the Apostles' Creed, and the Lord's Prayer. These comments constitute the heart of his *Short Exposition* (1520), a marvelous devotional writing Christians today can read with great profit.

At first it may seem strange to us that Luther emphasized the role of the Ten Commandments, the Creed, and the Lord's Prayer in the Christian's life, given his commitment to the entire Scripture. But any apparent incongruity disappears when we recall that Luther believed that those statements contained the whole substance of the Scriptures. Moreover, Luther had a rationale for their choice: in the Ten Commandments we discover what to do and what to leave undone; once we understand our inability to live the Christian life by our own means, we learn from the Creed where to find necessary strength; and in the Lord's Prayer, we learn "how to seek and obtain that strength."[12] Luther's admonition that Christians (especially non-readers) memorize the passages had been thought through carefully.

It should be noted also that Luther's appeal that the three items be memorized was not in itself innovative. During the Middle Ages the Roman Catholic church had urged the same, adding the Hail Mary to the list of those statements all Christians were to know by heart (*Writings II*, p. 13, n. 11). Luther did rearrange the order according to which the items should be considered in devotional reflection.

HOW TO PRAY AND MEDITATE

"All teachers of the Scriptures conclude that prayer is nothing else than the lifting up of heart or mind to God," Luther wrote (*Writings I*, p. 25). Luther regarded prayer as simply "real talking with God" (Holl, *Religion*, p. 88). Christians should want to commune with their heavenly Father who graciously provides for them in so many ways. Then again, as Luther noted, God requires Christians to pray: "He has not left it to our choice." The brute reality is, however, that many Christians do not pray. Luther put part of the blame for their failure to do so upon the devil's harrassment. Satan takes diabolical delight when

---

12. *Luther's Works: Devotional Writings II*, vol. 43, ed. Gustav K. Wiencke and Helmut T. Lehmann (Philadelphia: Fortress, 1968), p. 13; hereafter, *Writings II*.

Christians do not pray and meditate upon God's Word. He is constantly seeking to entice us away from prayer by one diversion or another: "The devil who besets us is not lazy or careless, and our flesh is too ready and eager to sin and is disinclined to the spirit of prayer" (*Writings II,* p. 194). Then again, Luther agreed with the monastic saying that no harder work exists than prayer. That fact should be frankly acknowledged in planning the Christian's devotional life.

With these things in mind, Luther took pains to encourage Christians to pray and, perhaps more important, gave instructions concerning how to pray. In "A Simple Way to Pray for a Good Friend, How One Should Pray, For Peter, the Master Barber," Luther with disarming candor reflected upon how he himself prayed:

> Dear Master Peter: I will tell you as best I can what I do personally when I pray. May our dear Lord grant to you and to everybody to do it better than I!
>
> (*Writings II,* p. 193)

In this marvelous piece to Peter and in other ones, Luther humbly offered his own experiences in prayer as suggestive models of what was good practice and what was bad.

For Luther, prayer and meditation were indispensable to the Christian's life. He saw prayer as being "the first business of the morning and last at night" (*Writings II,* p. 193). But Luther painfully confessed that sometimes he, too, did not want to pray. On such occasions he took definite remedial steps:

> First, when I feel that I have become cool and joyless in prayer because of other tasks or thoughts (for the flesh and devil always impede and obstruct prayer), I take my little psalter, hurry to my room, or, if it be the day and hour for it, to the church where a congregation is assembled and, as time permits, I say quietly to myself and word-for-word the Ten Commandments, the Creed, and, if I have time, some words of Christ or of Paul, or some psalms, just as a child might do.
>
> (*Writings II,* p. 193)

Ordinarily, however, a Christian's prayer life should not demand emergency measures.

In his *Large Catechism for Adults* (1529) Luther proposed a format for more routine devotions. The "Morning Blessing" of this catechism gives specific directions to the believer: a Christian is to get up from bed, make the sign of the cross, repeat the Creed and the Lord's Prayer while kneeling or standing, and perhaps close with this prayer:

I thank Thee, my heavenly Father, through Jesus Christ, Thy dear Son, that Thou hast preserved me through this night from all harm and danger, and I beseech Thee Thou wouldest protect me this day from sin and all evil, that all my deeds and my life may be pleasing in Thy sight. For I commend myself, my body and soul, and all, into Thy hands. Let Thy holy angel be with me, that the evil one may have no power over me. Amen.[13]

In the evening the Christian is to follow the same procedure (changing the appropriate words in the closing prayer). This devotional routine was well suited for the peasant or worker who did not know how to read. And certainly, readers might choose to use it if they were hurried.

It should be observed, however, that Luther hoped that a Christian might spend more time in spiritual reflection than that required for routine devotions. Luther's comments on a richer prayer and devotional life were quite extensive. They deserve our attention as well.

THE "GOOD PRAYERS" OF EXTENDED DEVOTIONS

Luther believed that the best definition of what he called "good" praying was praying that God hears and answers. Because Christians should want to know what makes their prayers good, Luther proposed several characteristics of such prayers.

First, a Christian who prays a good prayer does so with care and with singleness of heart. The Christian's mind should be prepared to concentrate upon what is prayed. Wrote Luther:

> It seems to me that if someone could see what arises as prayer from a cold and unattentive heart he would conclude that he had never seen a more ridiculous kind of buffonery.
>
> (*Writings II*, p. 199)

Second, in order to keep our minds from wandering, we should pray out loud:

> Indeed, no one should depend on his heart and presume to pray without uttering words unless he is well trained in the Spirit and has experience

13. Harry Bettenson, ed., *Documents of the Christian Church,* 2d ed. (New York: Oxford University Press, 1970), p. 208.

in warding off stray thoughts. Otherwise the devil will thoroughly trick him and soon smother the prayer in his heart. Therefore we should cling to the words and with their help soar upward, until our feathers grow and we can fly without the help of words.

(*Writings I*, p. 25)

Third, if a Christian concentrated in prayer, then he or she would remember what was prayed. That was important, for Luther believed good praying involved remembering what one had prayed:

But, praise God, it is now clear to me that a person who forgets what he has said has not prayed well. In a good prayer one fully remembers every word and thought from the beginning to the end of the prayer.

(*Writings II*, p. 199)

Fourth, Luther liked short prayers, not mindless, long-winded ones. A good prayer "must have few words, but be great and profound in content and meaning" (*Writings I*, p. 19). In the monastery Luther had encountered monks who could intone mechanically through long hours of prayer. For Luther, such prayers were nearly meaningless.

Fifth, a good prayer involved praying for others, not just for oneself. Luther paraphrased Chrysostom on this point: "All of Christendom prays for him who prays for it" (*Writings I*, p. 60). We are to share each other's burdens. Luther condemned the selfish Christian who did not pray for fellow church members and who did not try to meet their needs. He took great comfort in the fact that his brothers and sisters in the Lord prayed for him, just as he prayed for them and ministered to them.

Sixth, and a "thousand" times more important for Luther than the other points, a Christian prayed a good prayer when he believed God heard the prayer and would respond to it according to His good pleasure: "Only that prayer is acceptable which breathes a firm confidence and trust that it will be heard. . . . because of the reliable pledge and promise of God" (*Writings I*, p. 77). The person who prays without faith or who does so as if to test the heavenly waters shows his or her lack of trust, either in God's power, or in God's concern for His children:

The petitioner who doubts whether he is heard and prays as a kind of adventure to see if he will be heard or not is guilty on two counts. First, he nullifies his prayer. . . . Second, he treats his most faithful and true God as a liar and an unreliable person . . . and by his doubt robs God of his honor and his truthful name.

(Holl, *Religion,* p. 89, n. 62)

The way we pray, therefore, reveals what we actually think about God. It is a more accurate barometric reading than what we say we believe about Him.

Who can pray good prayers? Only those Christians who remember who they are and who trust their faithful God, was Luther's response.

> We pray after all because we are unworthy to pray. The very fact that we are unworthy and that we dare to pray confidently, trusting only in the faithfulness of God, makes us worthy to pray and to have our prayer answered.
>
> (*Writings I*, p. 89)

Luther's suggestions about good praying (and there were other ones besides those) are pertinent to Christians today. They should be evaluated and applied to our own prayer life.

THE LORD'S PRAYER

What kind of prayer is an ideal one for the Christian to pray? As might have been expected from the previous discussion, Luther's favorite was undoubtedly the Lord's Prayer.

> To this day I suckle at the Lord's Prayer like a child, and as an old man eat and drink from it and never get my fill. It is the very best prayer, even better than the psalter, which is so very dear to me.
>
> (*Writings II*, p. 200)

Luther recommended that in a Christian's extensive devotions, he or she should begin with the Lord's Prayer and meditate upon the meaning of each of its lines. Luther's own commentaries on the Lord's Prayer, based on his reflection upon its words, testify to the spiritual riches that can be mined by the Christian who does what Luther suggested.

But how do the characteristics of good praying accord with Luther's preference for meditation upon the words of the Lord's Prayer? When does a Christian pray for the needs of his neighbors, for example? In his *Short Exposition of the Decalogue, the Apostles' Creed and the Lord's Prayer* (1520), Luther explained the relationship between personal prayers and reflection upon the Lord's Prayer. After we have prayed the words, "Our Father who art in heaven," and after we have reflected upon their meaning, we are to turn to the principal seven petitions of the Lord's Prayer (Matt. 6:9-13, KJV). Our individual prayers are to be offered in conjunction with our meditation upon several of those petitions.

In relation to the first petition, "Hallowed be Thy Name," Luther wrote: "All the Psalms are in place in this petition, and all prayers in which God is praised, glorified, lauded, or thanked, together with the whole of the *Te Deum*."[14] In relation to the second petition, "Thy Kingdom Come," Luther wrote: "This petition includes all the psalms, verses, and prayers, in which we beseech God to give us grace and virtue" (1:93). In relation to the third petition, "Thy will be done on earth as it is in heaven," Luther wrote: "This petition includes also all the psalms, verses, and prayers which we offer in our hearts against sins and other enemies" (1:94). In relation to the fourth petition, "Give us this day our daily bread," Luther wrote: "This petition includes all the prayers and psalms on behalf of those who rule over us, and particularly those for protection against false teachers, and those on behalf of Jews, heretics, and all the wayward; also those on behalf of all who are afflicted, and all who suffer, knowing no consolation" (1:95). In relation to the fifth petition, "And forgive us our debts, as we forgive our debtors," Luther wrote: "This petition includes all the psalms and prayers which call on God for His mercy on our sins" (1:97). And finally, we are to conclude our meditation upon the Lord's Prayer and our petitions with these words:

> Grant, O God, a most certain answer to all these petitions, and let us not doubt that Thou has heard, and wilt hear, us when we offer them; and that, in answer, Thou wilt grant them and not refuse them, or leave us in doubt. So with joy we say: "Amen; it is true and assured." Amen.
>
> (Woolf, *Reformation Writings*, 1:99)

THE TEN COMMANDMENTS

If an individual has prayed and meditated upon the Lord's Prayer and there remains time for further communion with God, Luther proposed in his letter to Peter the barber that the Christian should turn his or her attention to the Ten Commandments. Each commandment could be beneficially approached from four different perspectives:

> That is, I think of each commandment as, first, instruction, which is really what it is intended to be, and consider what the Lord God demands of me so earnestly. Second, I turn it into a thanksgiving [ie., for what God has done for me]; third, a confession [ie., of my sin in terms of the commandment considered]; and fourth, a prayer [ie., for God's help to turn away from the evil spoken of in the commandment and to seek good].
>
> (*Writings II*, p. 200)

14. Woolf, *Reformation Writings*, 1:91. All quotations in this paragraph are from *Reformation Writings*; page numbers are given in parentheses.

For example, Luther treated the First Commandment in this fashion:

"I am the Lord your God," etc. "You shall have no other gods before me," etc. Here I earnestly consider that God expects and teaches me to trust him sincerely in all things and that it is his most earnest purpose to be my God. . . . Second, I give thanks for his infinite compassion by which he has come to me in such a fatherly way and, unasked, unbidden, and unmerited, has offered to be my God, to care for me. . . . Third, I confess and acknowledge my great sin and ingratitude for having so shamefully despised such sublime teachings. . . . Fourth, I pray and say: "O my God and Lord, help me by thy grace to learn and understand thy commandments more fully every day and to live by them in sincere confidence."

(*Writings II*, pp. 200–201)

THE APOSTLES' CREED

If, after having prayed through the Ten Commandments, time still remains for devotions, a person should turn to the Apostles' Creed and pray through it in much the same fashion as was done concerning the Ten Commandments. Such meditation would, as Luther picturesquely explained, "make it [the Apostles' Creed] into a garland of four strands" (*Writings II*, p. 209).

Obviously, Luther's extensive program for devotions and prayer would take a great deal of time to pursue, more than a Christian might have at his disposal on a given day. Luther was fully aware of that. He proposed that a believer might concentrate on whatever portion of the program that was spiritually meaningful to him on a particular day. If, for example, during reflective moments upon a portion of the Lord's Prayer, the Holy Spirit spoke to the believer through the Word, he should pause and go no further:

If such an abundance of good thoughts comes to us we ought to disregard the other petitions, make room for such thoughts, listen in silence, and under no circumstances obstruct them. The Holy Spirit himself preaches here, and one word of his sermon is far better than a thousand of our prayers. Many times I have learned more from one prayer than I might have learned from much reading and speculation.

(*Writings II*, p. 198)

In brief, Luther intended that his extensive format for a devotional life be used flexibly. He did not see it as a straitjacket:

I do not bind myself to such words or syllables, but say my prayers in one fashion today, in another tomorrow, depending upon my mood and feeling. I stay however, as nearly as I can, with the same general thoughts and ideas.

(*Writings II,* p. 198)

Rather it provided a helpful framework for keeping the Christian in daily contact with the Word of God. Moreover it was convenient; it was based on the same passages the people should have memorized as a matter of course: the Ten Commandments, the Apostles' Creed, and the Lord's Prayer.

DEVOTIONS AND A BUSY SCHEDULE

Luther took his own advice to heart. That is to say, Luther tried to spend as much time as he could in reflecting upon the Lord's Prayer, the Creed, and the Ten Commandments. The more crowded his schedule, the more time he wanted to spend in devotional preparation for the day's activities. He was only too cognizant of the temptations and the inconveniences of business. Luther fought to have time for his devotional life in his schedule. He arose early for prayer and meditation:

Do not think the catechism is a little thing to be read hastily and cast aside. Although I am a doctor, I have to do just as a child and say word for word every morning and whenever I have time the Lord's Prayer and the Ten Commandments, the Creed and the Psalms. I have to do it every day, and yet I cannot stand as I would.

(Bainton, *Life,* p. 264)

In the morning he lectured and preached; at 10:00 A.M. he ate the main meal of the day; in the afternoon he studied and wrote; at 5:00 P.M. he dined; in the evening he spent time in conversation and reading; at 9:00 P.M. he went to bed. Luther described his evening devotions in this fashion: "I have to hurry all day to get time to pray. It must suffice me if I can say the Ten Commandments, the Lord's Prayer, and one or two petitions besides, thinking of which I fall asleep."[15] Luther sometimes struggled to maintain a good devotional life, just as many of us do. But probably more than most Christians today, Luther was convinced that daily prayer and meditation upon God's Word afford the believer with spiritual nourishment and protection against the snares of Satan:

15. Cited in Preserved Smith, *The Life and Letters of Martin Luther* (London: John Murray, 1911), p. 317; hereafter Smith, *Life and Letters.*

To be occupied with God's Word helps against the world, the flesh, and the Devil, and all bad thoughts. This is the true holy water with which to exorcise the Devil.

(Bainton, *Life*, 264)

COPING WITH DESPAIR, DIFFICULTIES, AND THE DEVIL

For all his diligent care to walk with the Lord, Luther was not immune from depression, from losing bouts with the devil, and from sin. In 1527 he wrote: "For more than a week I was close to the gates of death and hell. I trembled in all my members. Christ was wholly lost. I was shaken by desperation and blasphemy of God" (Bainton, *Life*, pp. 282–83). Some psychologists have read much into Luther's struggles so as to make Luther appear to be a psychological cripple. That characterization is patently unfair, as Bainton and others have convincingly argued. Admittedly, Luther experienced dark and painful moments. He interpreted them, however, as those occasions that permitted him to understand God's grace better:

> If I live longer, I would like to write a book about *Anfechtungen* [assaults upon the soul], for without them no man can understand Scripture, faith, the fear or the love of God. He does not know the meaning of hope who was never subject to temptations.[16]

In a strange way that exceeds our comprehension, God permits what occurs to us to occur, even the bad (including the devil's attacks upon us). He does so with our good in mind. He does so with the intention of making us more like the image of His dear Son, Christ. If we can trust God, our heavenly Father, and give thanks to Him for our troubles and for the cross we bear daily, then we are growing in grace:

> For them [Christians] the holy cross serves for learning the faith, for [learning] the power of the word, and for subduing whatever sin and pride remain. Indeed, a Christian can no more do without the cross than without food or drink.[17]

Depressions and troubles, therefore, are far from being negative for the

16. Bainton, *Life*, p. 283. For a discussion of the concept of *Anfechtung*, see Holl, *Religion*, pp. 74–80. Luther viewed his opponent in these assaults as Satan or, sometimes, as God Himself.
17. *Writings II*, p. 184. Concerning Luther's detailed reflections on the cross, see Walther von Loewenich, *Luther's Theology of the Cross*, trans. Herbert J. Bowman (Minneapolis: Augsburg, 1976).

Christian. The way we cope with them gives another barometric reading of the level of our trust in our heavenly Father and of our growth in sanctification (or the working out of our baptism).

Until the very end of his life Luther bemoaned the troubles that the devil provokes in this world:

> Well, then, we oldsters simply have to live long enough to see the devil from the rear [see him for what he really is], having brought so much wickedness, treachery, and suffering upon the world. It is up to us to bear witness that the devil has been an evil influence.[18]

That does not mean that Luther found masochistic pleasure in his depressions, troubles, or combats with the devil. On the contrary, he gave much counsel to Christians about how they might deal with them. Concerning depression, Christ's words "Let not your heart be troubled" were decisive ones for Luther. A Christian was not to allow himself or herself to be mired in feelings of despondency:

> A Christian should and must be a cheerful person. If he isn't, the devil is tempting him. I have sometimes been grieviously tempted while bathing in my garden, and then I have sung the hymn "Let us now praise Christ." Otherwise I would have been lost then and there. Accordingly, when you notice that you have some such thoughts, say, "This isn't Christ." . . . Christ knows that our hearts are troubled, and it is for this reason that he says and commands, "Let not your hearts be troubled."[19]

Besides calling upon Christ, what can a Christian do specifically to overcome melancholy? Luther made many suggestions about this. Some of them might leave today's Christians a little uneasy; others are more recognizably helpful. Luther noted that depressed Christians should seek the good company of others:

> Having been taught by experience I can say how you ought to restore your spirit when you suffer from spiritual depression. When you are assailed by gloom, despair, or a troubled conscience you should eat, drink, and talk with others. If you can find help for yourself by thinking of a girl, do so.
>
> (Luther, *Table Talk*, pp. 17–18)

---

18. Cited in Justus Jonas, *The Last Days of Luther* (Garden City, N.Y.: Doubleday, 1970), p. 59.
19. *Luther's Works: Table Talk*, vol. 54., ed. Theodore G. Tappert and Helmut T. Lehmann; trans. Theodore G. Tappert (Philadelphia: Fortress, 1967), p. 96; hereafter, Luther, *Table Talk*. Luther gave much advice to correspondents concerning overcoming melancholy. See Tappert, *Letters*, pp. 89–98.

Or he recommended that the depressed Christian should listen to music:

> Music drives away the Devil and makes people gay.... I would not exchange what little I know of music for something great. Experience proves that next to the Word of God only music deserves to be extolled as the mistress and governess of the feelings of the human heart.
>
> (Bainton, *Life*, pp. 266-67)

> But my love for it [music] abounds; it has often refreshed me and freed me from great troubles.
>
> (Smith, *Life and Letters*, p. 347)

Or he suggested that a Christian might find joy through communion with the living Christ in the sacrament of the Lord's Supper. Rarely do we find in Luther the admonition "Buck up and try to be happy." Luther knew from personal experience in the monastery and elsewhere that attempts at self-induced happiness often end in failure. Far better is it for the person to think about the Person of Christ, to seek His help, to join the company of friends (especially the communion of saints, that is, caring church members), or to listen to the strains of soothing music.

Concerning coping with troubles, Luther had specific suggestions to make:

> First, ... a person must by no means rely on himself.... Rather, he must lay hold of the words offered to him in God's name, cling to them.... Second, he must not imagine that he is the only one assailed about his salvation.... Third, he should by no means insist on deliverance from these trials without yielding to the divine will.... Fourth, there is no stronger medicine for this than to begin with words such as David used when he said in Psalm 18, "I will call upon the Lord and praise him, and so shall I be saved from all that assails me." ... Fifth, he must thank God diligently for deeming him worthy of such a visitation, of which many thousands of people remain deprived.
>
> (*Writings I*, p. 183)

Once again, these principles are worthy of our careful consideration as Christians living in the twentieth century. They are not time-bound.

Concerning combat with the devil, Luther spoke out of painful experience. He confessed that his greatest temptations came when he was alone, when his mind was not occupied, and it wandered. Then the devil would assault him. On some occasions Luther stood his ground, claimed Christ's continuing victory over the devil, and told the evil one to be gone (Keppler, *Table Talk,* p. 6). More frequently, Luther found that it was wiser to flee the devil's intrigues by seeking company or by engaging in manual work. The devil was too clever to take on, one-on-one, during leisure time:

> Don't argue with the Devil. He has had five thousand years of experience. He has tried out all his tricks on Adam, Abraham, and David, and he knows exactly the weak spots.[20]

Flight was better than fight. Luther bore the battle scars to prove the folly of solo combat.

Throughout his productive life as a Reformer, Luther found himself caught up in rude spiritual warfare. We often forget that he lived under that punishing condition. His accomplishments became thereby all the more impressive. For him, the devil was no red-tunicked imp, pitchfork in hand, of dubious storybook fame. Rather, the devil was that much alive, perfidious creature who busily sought Luther's own ruin by plunging him into depression, or by disrupting his communion with his heavenly Father, the author of his salvation and of all peace. In such circumstances a healthy devotional life was critically important to Luther. He took pains to explain it to fellow Christians, for it provided a front line defense against Satan, it bolstered the believer's ability to cope with troubles, and it could bring the Christian under the shelter of a "Mighty Fortress," who is, as Luther the songwriter celebrated, "Our God":

> And though this world, with devils filled, should threaten to undo us;
> We will not fear, for God hath willed His truth to triumph through us:
> The Prince of Darkness grim, We tremble not for him; His rage we can endure,
> For lo, his doom is sure, One little word shall fell him.

LUTHER'S COUNSEL AND EXAMPLE: AN APPRAISAL

Few Christians would deny that the Lord God used Martin Luther singularly in the reform of His church. As a result, Luther often casts an image bigger than life on the screens of our minds. We can scarcely imagine that he was molded out of human clay, just as we are. And yet, our brief survey reveals a very human Luther, valiantly battling with

---

20. Bainton, *Life,* p. 284. See also Luther's instructions for driving away the devil from a believer (Tappert, *Letters,* p. 52).

the infirmities of the flesh, becoming deeply discouraged, and losing some rounds with the devil along the way. Despite all that, his stout-hearted trust in his heavenly Father generally remained unshaken. Probably for that reason God could use him significantly to stir His church. Luther had, and had been given, the faith about which he spoke so much.

What is so particularly attractive about Luther is his evangelical pastor's heart. Even though he was busy writing, studying, and organizing, Luther demonstrated great compassion for his family, friends, and followers. He devoted as much time as he could to providing them with good counsel concerning how they might know God better and walk with Him. His advice and modeling were as precious as fine gold in that he, a frail human being, knew God well and wrote and spoke as one who had experienced what he proclaimed. Over and over again, in giving his advice, Luther referred to his own experiences of God's faithfulness and patience with him. He wanted other Christians to have confidence in and love for the God who is really there, their heavenly Father. Luther put the matter in this practical way:

> God wants us to look to him as our God and Father in Christ, to call upon him in every time of need and to be confident that he will provide for us, as St. Peter says, quoting Psalm 55 [:22], "Cast all your anxieties on him for he cares about you" [1 Peter 5:7], and as Christ himself says, Matthew 6 [:31], "You should not be anxious."
>
> (*Writings II*, p. 174)

Today, we are not bound to follow Martin Luther's counsel or his example in all matters. Some aspects of his theology we may prefer to disregard. Non-Lutherans, for example, may not appreciate Luther's emphasis upon the sacraments. And certainly most of us will want to leave aside certain intemperate vocabulary and behavior of the famous Saxon. Nonetheless, we can benefit immeasurably by sorting through and applying many of Luther's doctrinal teachings and practical suggestions to our walk with God.

In a media-saturated world where so much non-Christian modeling parades before us, seeking to beguile us and have us forget our God and His Christ, we do well to turn to Martin Luther. Here is a person who knew God and loved God. Here is a person who, at least in certain areas of his life, affords us excellent Christian modeling by word and deed. But in considering the German Reformer, we should always recall that our supreme example is the God-man, Christ Jesus, and not a man, Martin Luther. With that, Martin Luther would have heartily concurred. Although he appreciated the godly saints who had come before him, his ultimate example was Christ Jesus. Luther expressed that sentiment with the beauty that often accompanies simplicity:

> The heavenly image is Christ, who was a man full of love, mercy, and grace, meekness, patience, wisdom, light, and all good, whose very nature was to serve all men and harm none. This image we must also carry; we must be like Him.
>
> (Preus, *Theology,* 69)

8 Putting the Renewed Mind to Work

Douglas Moo

I knew I had a problem when I could barely force my car door open—the car had tilted over that far. Intent on looking at a new house, I had driven off the side of the road, and my car had become embedded up to the axle in soft mud. It took the winch on a tow truck to extricate my car from its predicament.

Christians face a similar predicament as they strive to "take captive every thought to make it obedient to Christ" (2 Corinthians 10:5, NIV). Our minds are stuck in a rut, a pattern of thinking that is antagonistic to the will of God. Successful Christian living depends on our getting out of that rut and establishing another, one that is characterized by biblical values and ways of thinking. It is this need that Paul expresses in perhaps the most famous of all New Testament texts about the Christian mind, Romans 12:2 (quoted here in the forceful paraphrase by J. B. Phillips): "Don't let the world around you squeeze you into its own mold, but let God remold your minds from within, so that you may prove in practice that the plan of God for you is good, meets all his demands and moves toward the goal of true maturity."

But it is significant that Paul does not stop there. He goes on to speak of the purpose of the renewal of the mind: "to test and approve what

Douglas Moo (B.A., DePauw University; M. Div., Trinity Evangelical Divinity School; Ph.D., University of St. Andrews, Scotland) is associate professor of New Testament at Trinity Evangelical Divinity School. He has written *The Old Testament* in the *Gospel Passion Narratives* and is co-author of *The Rapture: Pre-, Mid-, or Post-Tribulational?*

God's will is—his good, pleasing and perfect will" (NIV). What does it mean to test or approve the will of God? John Murray offers this fine explanation: It means

> to discover, to find out or learn by experience what the will of God is. It is a will that will never fail or be found wanting. If life is aimless, stagnant, fruitless, lacking in content, it is because we are not entering by experience into the richness of God's will. The commandment of God is exceedingly broad. There is not a moment of life that the will of God does not command, no circumstance that it does not fill with meaning if we are responsive to the fullness of his revealed counsel for us.[1]

The renewal of the mind should lead to the practice of God's will in all areas of life.

What does the New Testament have to say about the application of the mind to day-to-day living? Are there guidelines for the Christian to follow as he grapples with the challenges of a complex world? And how can he actually go about putting the renewed mind to work? Those and other questions provide the agenda for this essay.

GUIDELINES FOR THE RENEWED MIND

The first question to be asked is this: What guidelines are there to help us in determining what it is we are to do? It is often suggested that the leading of the renewed mind itself is sufficient; that Christians need nothing more than the internal witness of the indwelling Spirit to direct their thoughts and actions. Certainly the New Testament strongly emphasizes the role of the Holy Spirit in directing the steps of the believer. Jesus promised that he would send "the Counselor, the Holy Spirit" to "teach you all things" (John 14:25–26, NIV). And Paul says to the Galatians: "Live by the Spirit, and you will not gratify the desires of your sinful nature" (Gal. 5:16, NIV). But it is important to recognize that the New Testament does not stop there. In the same passage in which He promised the gift of the Spirit, Jesus also told his disciples: "Whoever has my commands and obeys them, he is the one who loves me" (John 14:21, NIV). And Paul, the great apostle of freedom in the Spirit, reminded the wayward Corinthians that "keeping God's commands is what counts" (1 Cor. 7:19, NIV). In fact, in the New Testament the internal, renewing work of the Holy Spirit is stressed side-by-side with a constant concern for obedience to external commands. As people who have been redeemed but not yet glorified,

1. *The Epistle to the Romans* (Grand Rapids: Eerdmans, 1965), 2:115.

Christians need both. As powerful as is the Spirit, He indwells people who still possess sinful natures. Reliance on the Spirit alone, with no external guidelines, quickly leads to an enthronement of the individual ego. I do what I do because it seems good to me—ignoring the fact that I do not have perfect knowledge of God. No one saw the imperfect nature of the Christian more clearly than did Luther. He called the believer one who is "at the same time justified and a sinner." And because of that, he forcefully proclaimed the Christian's continuing need for external guidance.

So the Christian is guided, in this practical outworking of the Christian mind, by commands. But what commands? This is not the place to deal with such a thorny issue in any detail. Suffice to say that the New Testament focuses on the commands given by Jesus and repeated and explained by the apostles. As his last charge, Jesus commanded his disciples to teach baptized converts "to obey everything *I* have commanded you" (Matt. 28:20, NIV; emphasis added). Throughout his ministry, Jesus authoritatively taught his disciples the will of God. And although believers today must be careful not to apply to themselves what Jesus meant only for those first disciples, the teaching of Jesus gives to Christians a rich store of commands for daily life. Paul himself referred to the teaching of Jesus in giving guidance to his churches (see 1 Cor. 7:10; 9:14). More often, however, Paul advised his churches on the basis of his own apostolic authority. Those commands can furnish the individual believer as well with concrete guidelines for the direction of the Christian mind. Throughout the New Testament, we see a similar situation. The inspired authors issued commands to their first century hearers, commands that have been preserved for us as a rich, variegated source for guidance. Again, not everything they said can be directly applied to the present circumstances: situations change and some of the New Testament authors' advice was intended only for their own situations. But judicious application of good principles of interpretation (hermeneutics) will usually enable the reader to distinguish clearly what was intended only for the first century and what was intended as timeless advice to Christians everywhere, at any time.

All this is very well, it might be objected, but doesn't Paul himself say that Christians "are not under law, but under grace" (Rom. 6:14)? Isn't it trying to put Christians back under the law to say that they must obey specific commands? It is true that Paul proclaimed Christians to be free from the law. But what law was he referring to? Even a casual reading of Paul's letters shows that usually he used this word *law* to refer to the Mosaic law, that particular body of commands given to Israel at the time of the ratification of the Sinaitic covenant. For instance, Paul said that the law was given four hundred and thirty years after Abraham (Gal. 3:17) and that before Moses there was "no law" (Rom. 5:13-14). What Paul meant, in other words, when he said that Christians were not "under law" was that they were no longer "held prisoners" (Gal. 3:23, NIV; see also Rom. 7:6) by the Mosaic law. The era in which the old covenant held sway had passed; with the coming of Christ, a new covenant had begun. Christians belonged to that new covenant. Certainly many old covenant commands were applicable to Christians: Paul quoted at least one of them as authoritative for believers (Eph. 6:2-3) and every one of the Ten Commandments, except the Sabbath command, is repeated in the New Testament. But as a system, the old covenant law no longer ruled the believer. He was now under the "law of Christ" (1 Cor. 9:21; Gal. 6:2), the "royal law" (James 2:8), "the perfect law that gives freedom" (James 1:25, NIV), the "new commandment" that Jesus gave (John 13:34). Therefore, it is vital to recognize that the believers' freedom is freedom from *the* law, not *all* law. Believers must meet God's demands in a new context, but God's demands they are.

One other objection to the idea that Christians are obliged to obey specific commands should be mentioned. It is this: Christians are not obligated to commands but to a command—the love command. Jesus himself summarized the demand of God in this one, new command (John 13:34). Paul claimed that "the whole law" was fulfilled in the command to love one's neighbor as oneself (Gal. 5:13-14; Rom. 13:8-10); James identified the "royal law, according to the Scripture" as the same command (2:8). All we need is love, many proclaim; as long as we love, anything we do must be moral. That approach, sometimes called the "new morality," is popular, both within and outside the church. It exerts a strong appeal on a generation that is uncomfortable with absolutes, that would like to be free from conventional moral codes, that proclaims "I'm OK, you're OK." To such persons, right and wrong cannot be laid out in black and white; what is right in one situation might be wrong in another, and vice versa. Motivation is the only absolute. If I do what I do out of love for others, it is right.

Now there is certainly a germ of truth in that approach. It is accurate to say that the New Testament consistently highlights love as the essence and summary of God's commands. But this love, according to Jesus, has an object prior to, and infinitely higher than, man: " 'Love the Lord your God with all your heart, with all your soul, and with all your mind.' This is the first and greatest commandment" (Matt. 22:37, NIV). And how do we love God? "This is love for God: to obey his commands" (1 John 5:3, NIV). Genuine Christian love is focused, first and foremost, on God our creator and redeemer. And true love for God means a radical commitment to obey all that He tells us. As love is the greatest command, so obedience to God's commands is the greatest, deepest, most authentic expression of that love. Yes, love for the neighbor is the essence and summary of the law. But it does not exhaust the law, either the Mosaic law or the "law of Christ." If love were really all that was needed, why would Paul have spent so much time giving his churches concrete, specific commands? It needs to be understood that neither Jesus, nor Paul, nor James intended to set up love for the neighbor as the only command. What they did was to single out love as the greatest, the most important, the single clearest expression of the commands God gives men. It is, Jesus reminds us, one of "the weightier matters" (Matt. 23:23, RSV*). But it is not the only matter. In their sin and weakness, men too easily mistake love for selfishness; they too readily fool themselves into doing what they want out of so-called humanitarian motives. The love that should characterize all that men do needs to be guided. The internal motive of love works together with the external demands of God's law. No one can truly love his neighbor unless he loves God at the same time.

The importance of obedience to God's commands for the direction of the renewed mind has been stressed so far in this essay, because many Christians are ignoring the importance of those commands. But once believers see that they are to be guided by specific external commands, they must move on to the recognition of the place of the internal, the Spirit-filled heart and renewed mind, in the process of determining what behavior will please God. It is this side of the picture that Paul had in mind when he commanded the Ephesians to "understand what the Lord's will is" (Eph. 5:17, NIV). Similarly, Paul prayed that the love of the Philippians might "abound more and more in knowledge and depth of insight, so that you may be able to discern what is best and may be pure and blameless until the day of Christ" (Phil. 1:9-10, NIV). The Christian faces many situations in which the Word of God gives no specific command. What is needed in such situations is the ability to apply the general guidelines of Scripture to those specific circumstances.

As believers grow in Christ, they will become increasingly sensitive to the will of the Lord, and the Spirit continually will be merging the direction of their will with the will of God. Another word that might be

Revised Standard Version.

applied to the matter of obedience is the word wisdom. In the same context of Ephesians mentioned above, Paul exhorted the believers to "be careful, then, how you live—not as unwise, but as wise" (5:15, NIV). In Scripture wisdom does not refer so much to intellectual knowledge as to spiritual discernment and values. James said that this wisdom is "first of all pure, then peace-loving, considerate, submissive, full of mercy and good fruit, impartial and sincere" (3:17, NIV). The person who lives by those values is the one who is wise and who will be able to discern the right thing in any situation. This wisdom, as both Proverbs 2:6 and James 1:5 stress, is given by God and can be received by "[asking] in faith" (James 1:5-8).

In sum, then, the New Testament pictures as the ideal the believer whose heart and mind are so closely aligned with God's will that he automatically does what is right. Such a renewed mind is a crucial source for the guidance of the believer's thinking and actions. But the New Testament also makes clear that the renewed mind never becomes perfectly renewed in this life, but is always in the process of being more and more transformed. Thus, the external, specific commands of the "law of Christ" remain as the authoritative, indispensible guide to the renewed mind. One should not be set against the other: the renewal of the mind is to be guided by God's commands. God's commands are to be applied to specific circumstances through the wisdom that comes from the renewed mind.

CHARACTERISTICS OF THE RENEWED MIND

The new pattern of thinking that begins with conversion must undergo a constant process of renewal. In the building of this Christian mind, the commands of God in Scripture provide a basic blueprint, while the redeemed, Spirit-filled mind itself applies those commands in certain situations. But what are the specific concrete values and actions that should characterize people who have renewed minds? Where do some of the particular problems lie for believers today who are trying to think and act "Christianly"? Obviously, many problems could be cited. But the slogan "the me generation" captures particularly well the essence of the problem in the present day. Even secular social critics, such as Christopher Lasch in *The Culture of Narcissism* (New York: W. W. Norton, 1979), have seen that. Indeed, Scripture suggests that, in one form or another, pride, or selfishness, has always been a root sin. But as believers go about the task of developing genuinely Christian ways of looking at life, can they pinpoint specific areas in which selfishness is likely to manifest itself in their lives? There are five areas the Scripture has much to say about.

THE SELF AND AUTHORITY

As a college student, I lived through perhaps the most anti-authoritarian era in American history: the late 1960s, with anti-Vietnam war rallies, countercultures, and rebellion. Many social critics have commented on the fact that that movement has now passed; Americans, especially young Americans, are now working within the system to advance their own interests. But this new semblance of the acceptance of authority has strictly defined, essentially utilitarian, limits: Submit to authority as long as its rewards outweigh its penalties. If you can get away with it, and it helps you, do it.

Christians are not immune from such trends. The tendency to obey only as long as it is easy or rewarding is deeply ingrained. Yet the New Testament stresses that the believer lives in a number of different authority relationships, and that his obedience to those authorities does not depend on convenience or whim. Four authority situations in particular are given attention in the New Testament: God, government, church, and family.

That Christians are to obey God in all that he commands probably goes without saying. Yet Christians need to remind themselves that God's commands are uncompromising and unchanging. They must beware subtle pressures to redefine the demands of God in order to make them easier to obey. To be sure, the believer must always be careful to apply accepted standards of interpretation and avoid taking everything in a literalistic manner. But more often the problem is that Christians shape their interpretation of Scripture to suit their wishes. If God is truly to be authoritative in the lives of believers, they must allow His word to speak to them, to direct them, to change them. It must judge them, not they it.

As Christians render "to God the things that are God's," they must also be careful to "render to Caesar the things that are Caesar's" (Matt. 22:21). The new Testament plainly requires the Christian to be submissive to governing authorities (see Rom. 13:1-7; Titus 3:1-2; 1 Pet. 2:13-17). Certainly there is a limit to what government can force the Christian to do. When the authorities commanded Peter and John to stop preaching Christ, they refused (Acts 4:17-20). But the principle seems to be that Christians can refuse to obey government only when a violation of the Spirit-led conscience of the believer would be caused. Again, the tendency too often is to justify disobedience of secular laws simply because it would be helpful to one or because one can probably get away with it. Cheating on tax returns, it seems, is endemic. Christians, however, are required to be scrupulously honest in filling out those returns; to list all their income, whether the IRS can find out about it or not!

The church, and its leaders, is a third authority structure in which the believer lives. Paul tells the Thessalonian Christians "to respect those who labor among you and are over you in the Lord and admonish you" (1 Thess. 5:12, RSV). The church at Corinth was told by Paul to take decisive action against one of its members who was committing a gross sin (1 Cor. 5:1-7). Believers are to submit willingly to church discipline as a means of correcting error and preserving the purity of the church. Certainly many Christians belong to churches where such discipline would be unheard of, but that is another problem. The point is that Christians should be willing to accept the reproof of fellow-believers; indeed, they should welcome such reproof as an aid in avoiding sin.

Perhaps the most controversial area of authority in our day is the family. Probably no institution in American life has changed so quickly, or so radically, as the family. Certainly, the traditional family structure was closer to the biblical norm than what now seems to be popular. Therefore, as the Christian works at applying the renewed mind to his family relations, he must guard against some of the prevailing tendencies. One such tendency is to disrupt or deny the lines of authority in the family. The New Testament makes plain that wives are to submit willingly and graciously to husbands (Eph. 5:22; Col. 3:18; 1 Pet. 3:1-6) and that children are to obey their parents (Eph. 6:2-3; Col. 3:20). It is true that this teaching has often been abused. But abuse of a teaching does not justify abandoning that teaching. Believers need to avoid the pressure to make the Bible conform to the direction of their culture. The New Testament lays down clear guidelines for the functioning of the family, and the authority relationships within that structure are important.

THE SELF AND OTHERS

Loving one's neighbor as one loves one's self is a basic, frequently repeated, many-sided demand in the New Testament. It has as many applications as the people and situations we encounter. Loving others as one's self requires a willingness to take one's own interests and wants out of first place. When Paul wrote the epistle to the Philippians, the church at Philippi was apparently experiencing internal conflicts.

Paul encouraged the Christians there to be "like-minded, having the same love, being of one spirit and purpose" (Phil. 2:2, NIV). And what would provide the basis for such unity? A proper understanding of the place of the self in relation to others: "Do nothing out of selfish ambition or vain conceit, but in humility consider others better than yourselves. Each of you should look not only to your own interests, but also to the interests of others" (2:3–4, NIV).

One of the clearest manifestations of the Me Generation is its emphasis on self-fulfillment. In itself, of course, there is nothing wrong with that. Everyone should strive to develop his God-given potential to the best of his ability. But what has happened is that self-fulfillment has gone hand in hand with disregard for the interests and needs of others. Many situations in which that is true could be mentioned, but two will do. Granted the economic realities of the present day, it is not surprising that many mothers find it necessary to take jobs outside the home. But their motivation for doing so must be carefully examined. Is the job economically necessary, or simply economically helpful? Is the mother pursuing her own self-fulfillment at the expense of the needs of her children? Is the desire for a higher standard of living, for a few extra luxuries, being elevated over the emotional and spiritual needs of children? Those questions are not asked to condemn working mothers, but to point out one way in which the focus on self can harm others. The same problem afflicts the father whose desire to get ahead or to develop his own potential leads him to spend too much time at the office, the health club, or the golf course, and too little time at home.

Concern with the self has a far more serious manifestation. Many women who get abortions do so simply and admittedly because the child growing in the womb is an inconvenience to her or to her spouse. The rights of the child, the sanctity of that human life, are shunted aside in the interests of the parents. Is not something similar beginning to happen in the attitudes of many toward the elderly, the infirm, the handicapped, the terminally ill? Does the impetus for "pulling the plug" come from genuine concern for an individual who is suffering, or from the worry that the continued life of such an individual is getting in the way of plans, of a career, or of pleasures? Difficult questions are bound up with these issues, and they should not be discounted. But cavalier disregard for human life is often deeply rooted in nothing more than selfishness.

A more subtle manifestation of selfishness with respect to others can occur, strangely enough, among dedicated Christians. Their strong desire to grow in their faith can result in a one-sided emphasis on their own personal development at the expense of others in the church. That was one of the main problems in the Corinthian church. They gloried in their own wisdom, but, as a result, there were disputes in the church (1 Cor. 1-4). They prided themselves on their freedom in the Lord ("Everything is permissible for me"), but were neglecting the needs of others ("but not everything is edifying," 1 Cor. 6:12; 10:23, NIV). They valued spiritual gifts according to their personal value instead of according to their value in edifying the church as a whole (1 Cor. 14:1-12). Faced with this intensely individualistic Christianity, Paul reminded the Corinthian believers of their responsibility for others in the body (1 Cor. 8:9-13; 10:31 — 11:1). It is no accident that the great "love" chapter is found in 1 Corinthians: "Love ... is not self-seeking" (13:4-5, NIV). Without diminishing by one wit the desire Christians have as individuals to grow in faith, recognition must be given to the notion that true Christian growth involves an increase in one's ability and desire to serve others as well as in an increase in personal godliness.

THE SELF AND THE BODY

That selfishness can create serious problems in sexual morality is also clear from 1 Corinthians. Some in that church apparently felt they were so spiritual that it was wrong for them to have anything to do with sex at all. Paul reminded them that it was perfectly appropriate for Christians to marry and that it was necessary for sex be a part of that relationship (7:2-5). And he also stressed that the "one flesh" union of man and wife (Gen. 2:24) meant that the body of each individual belonged as much to the spouse as to the self (7:4). Sex in marriage was intended as a means of mutual pleasure and fulfillment, not of self-gratification.

Christians can err also in failing to recognize that God has a claim on their bodies and that that claim has far-reaching implications for sexual conduct. "The body is not meant for sexual immorality, but for the Lord, and the Lord for the body"; "Do you not know that your bodies are members of Christ himself?" (1 Cor. 6:13, 15, NIV).

If some Corinthians were taking the view that their new spiritual life made sexual expression inappropriate, others thought that it made sexual conduct unimportant. As long as a person's spirit belonged to the Lord, what did it matter what he did with his body? Few people today would justify sexual immorality on such grounds, but surely everyone is aware that the problem of sexual misconduct is a particularly serious one in this culture. In that respect, first-century society was not much different. The serious moral demands of the Christian faith clashed head-on with the loose standards characteristic of Roman society. Then, as now, Christians had to realize that "the body is . . . for the Lord" (6:13). And God's standards for the body are clear. Paul asserted that "neither the sexually immoral nor idolators nor adulterers not male prostitutes nor homosexual offenders . . . will inherit the kingdom of God" (1 Cor. 6:9-10, NIV). The Greek word *pornoi,* translated "sexually immoral," was a broad term that included a variety of sexual sins; sex before marriage was almost certainly one of those. Sex outside of marriage was condemned in the term "adulterers," while the last words included all forms of homosexual relationships. In other words, the verse unambiguously condemned sexual practices that are becoming increasingly accepted in American society today — even by some who call themselves Christians. Faced with the growing toleration of sexual sin, Christians should be scrupulously careful to be sure that their sexual values and morals are being formed by God's Word, not by the environment in which they live.

And they must keep in mind that the formation of sexual values involves much more than simply refraining from practices the Scripture forbids. Jesus made abundantly clear that sexual lust is a matter first, and most basically, of the mind and the heart: "I tell you that anyone who looks at a woman lustfully has already committed adultery with her in his heart" (Matt. 5:28, NIV). The practice of sexual sin is usually the inevitable culmination of a long tolerance of the idea of that sin in the heart. In order to guard themselves against the strong, swift current of sexual immorality, believers must be careful to anchor themselves to biblical values, to cultivate minds and hearts that are free from lustful thoughts. Our bodies have been given us by God; they will be redeemed by God. Believers are not their own. They have been "bought at a price." "Therefore," Paul continued, they should "honor God with [their bodies]" (1 Cor. 6:20).

THE SELF AND MONEY

That money and possessions represent a potent source of selfishness needs hardly to be said. Interestingly, Paul referred to money (6:10) immediately after castigating the sexually immoral (6:9). "Neither . . . the greedy . . . nor swindlers will inherit the kingdom of God" (1 Cor. 6:9-10). Probably everyone has been reminded often of the dangers of materialism. But abundant evidence exists that the warning is not being heeded within the church to the extent it should be. Indeed, there is danger of a reaction setting in. Some of the Christian social critics who have done the most to make believers aware of the dangers of materialism have perhaps gone to an extreme in advocating specific social and political remedies. Many have reacted against such teaching by reasserting support for other social and political values and systems. The danger is that the important message for the individual believer concerning wealth will get lost in the crossfire. What is that message?

Very simply, it is that one's money, like his body, is not his own. That does not mean that a person should have no possessions of his own. Though the early church in Jerusalem experimented with an unconstrained pooling of resources (Acts 2:44-45), no other church in the New Testament followed its example. Rather, what is necessary is that Christians make decisions about the use of money on the basis of the principles of the gospel. Love for the neighbor, compassion for the needy, concern for the priority of God's work—those are the factors that should mold the Christian's financial decisions. The constant danger is to make those decisions solely on the basis of one's perceived needs and desires. James was perhaps bolder on the subject of misusing wealth than any other New Testament author. He warned his readers that their prayers were going unanswered because of the attitude of their heart: "You ask with wrong motives, that you may spend what you get on your pleasures" (4:3, NIV). And, in a biting attack on the misuse of wealth, he pronounced judgment on the rich because they hoarded their wealth, defrauded their workers, and were concerned only with providing for their own luxurious life-style (5:1-6). Christians in modern America need to recapture James's perspective on wealth. They need constantly to remind themselves that money is not an end in itself, but is a means of providing for themselves and for serving others. They need to be careful to define their needs by biblical standards, not by the standards of their neighbors or by television commercials. They must live in a way that will show materialistic Americans that people can be truly happy without every single element of the American Dream. They need to demonstrate with their money that they really do love their neighbors more than themselves.

THE SELF AND TIME

I hesitate to mention this last area of selfishness because the New Testament does not say much about it, at least directly. The importance of submitting to authority, the need to elevate concern for others above oneself, the dangers of sexual immorality and greed—they are all repeatedly emphasized in the New Testament. But about the only passages that speak directly to the issue of time management are the passing comments of Paul about "making the most of every opportunity" (Eph. 5:16, NIV; Col. 4:5). Indirectly, however, in its comments about the believer's responsibility to be a loving, caring family member, fellow-Christian, and neighbor, the Bible has much to say about the use of time.

I know personally how easy it is to be selfish about time. After a long, hard day at work, it is easy for me to imagine that I have earned time of my own. But under the lordship of Christ, is there really any time that is mine? Can I ever be justified in deciding to use my time without regard for the Lord and others? This is not to say that any time I spend on my own, pursuing my own pleasures, is wrong. It is to say that my choices concerning time should be made with respect for biblical values and principles. They should not be based on narrow, selfish desires for self-fulfillment or on the notion that somehow I have a certain percentage of hours every day that belong only to me.

In the contemporary craze for self-development (witness the enormous number of self-help and hobby books rolling off the presses), Christians must be careful not to put their own development ahead of the development of their families or their churches. Time that could be spent reading or playing tennis could be spent with one's children or with one's spouse; or it could be spent at a church meeting or in study of God's Word. The needs of others should be given priority. Time for relaxing, for meditating, for thinking, and for exercising is important and necessary; God does not want anyone to burn himself out. What He wants is for Christians to cultivate a use of their time that reflects God's priorities rather than their own. Attention to God's priorities may mean that a Christian will spend more time in family recreation, in meditation, and in the cultivation of his mind than his secular friends will.

DEVELOPING THE RENEWED MIND

We have looked at the guidelines for the renewed mind—God's commands in Scripture and the Spirit-created wisdom that God gives us. We have seen areas of life in which the renewed mind should make a difference in the world we live in. But we are left with the all-important question: How do we go about doing this? How can we avoid becoming "conformed to the world"? How can we rise above ourselves and our ingrained selfishness? I have no magical key, infallible solution, or "seven sure steps" to offer. But I think Scripture does have several things to say about this "how" that are important.

We begin, naturally, with the Holy Spirit. When a person becomes a

Christian, not only does he enter into a new relationship with God, but God, by his Spirit, enters him. Far from being a person imprisoned in his own sinful, fallen nature, he is now indwelt by God's Spirit and is free to love and serve God, to produce "the fruit of the Spirit" (Gal. 5:22). That is where the "how" of the Christian life begins—with the transforming power of God's Spirit in the heart and mind. Romans 8:5-8 gives prominent place to "the mind controlled by the Spirit" (NIV), the mind that is aligned with the desires of the Spirit. But the process is far from being automatic. People are not trees which automatically produce fruit; they are creatures with a will, a will that is capable of rebelling against control of the mind by the Spirit. The New Testament recognizes that and pictures the Christian life as a life of growth and development. Paul said, "We, who with unveiled faces all reflect the Lord's glory, are being transformed into his likeness with ever-increasing glory, which comes from the Lord, who is the Spirit" (2 Cor. 3:18, NIV). Paul himself "[pressed] on to take hold of that for which Christ Jesus" had taken hold of him (Phil. 3:12). He encouraged Timothy to work hard, to exercise discipline, to "endure hardship" (2 Tim. 2:3-7, NIV).

Christians tend to move toward two extremes in this matter. Either they think that they can lie back and let God's spirit automatically produce Christian maturity, or they think that they, by clever programs or strenuous exertion, will succeed by main force in becoming perfect. Scripture, of course, combines these perspectives. In a verse that summarized a major discussion of the Christian life, Paul promised that "if by the Spirit" the believer was "putting to death the deeds of the body," he would live (Rom. 8:13; compare NIV). The believer, the acting, willing individual, is, indeed, to do something, but he can do it only "by the Spirit." The point to be made is that the indwelling Spirit, by Himself, does not guarantee a truly renewed mind. Christians must actively and constantly develop, mature, and practice what the Spirit has given them.

How can a Christian facilitate the process of training the renewed mind, the mind of the Spirit? The key would seem to be environment. What are the influences, the atmosphere in which his mind is being formed? What is determining the direction of his thinking? How ironic it is that many Christian parents who are concerned about the kind of school environment in which their children are being trained are completely unconcerned about or even unconscious of the environment that affects their own way of thinking. A mind that is exposed constantly to a barrage of secular television, secular advertising, secular literature, and secular ideas is probably going to turn out to be a secular mind. It is extraordinarily difficult for a person to resist the pressure to let his own values and beliefs be molded by those influences. Yet many Christians seem to be totally unaware that that it what is happening.

The Christian can reduce the power of the secular in his mind. He can do so not necessarily by cutting himself off from the secular world, although it is understandable why many Christians say that television, for example, presents so powerful and dangerous an influence that it might be best to avoid it altogether. Rather, what is important is that he be careful to expose himself to Christian resources that are able to mold his mind. He should avail himself of scriptural teaching, in a variety of forms. God's Word possesses the power to change one's thinking, to develop a distinctly Christian mind-set in a person. But that cannot happen unless he places himselves in an environment in which the Word is prominent. Daily study of Scripture, participation in Bible studies, regular church attendance, reading of Christian literature, even listening to Christian music, all are part of that environment. Then, armed with a biblical world view, the Christian can evaluate the other influences about him. Paul told the believers in Colossae to "let the word of God dwell in you richly as you teach and counsel one another with all wisdom, and as you sing psalms, hymns and spiritual songs with gratitude in your hearts to God" (Col. 3:16, NIV). That Word will be able to dwell in believers "richly" only if they come in contact with it constantly.

Just as we who are believers should be concerned about the factors influencing our thinking, so, too, should we be concerned about the direction of our thinking. "Whatever is lovely, whatever is admirable—if anything is excellent or praiseworthy—think about such things" (Phil. 4:8, NIV). As those who have been joined to Jesus Christ, "[sitting] at the right hand of God" (Acts 2:33), God has "seated us with him in the heavenly realms" (Eph. 2:6, NIV). We have been made citizens of heaven (Phil. 3:20). That new spiritual identity must always be uppermost in our thinking. We are "strangers here" (1 Pet. 1:17, NIV); our true home is the heavenly realm, with its distinctive values and laws. Our thinking should conform to that new identity. "Set your minds on the things above, not on earthly things" (Col. 3:2, NIV). The renewed mind is a mind that is formed by, and focused on, the unseen spiritual world to which we belong by faith. The more we understand and identify with the things of that world, the more our minds will be transformed. We will let Paul's prayer for the Colossians be our closing prayer:

For this reason, since the day we heard about you, we have not stopped praying for you and asking God to fill you with the knowledge of his will through all spiritual wisdom and understanding. And we pray this in order that you may live a life worthy of the Lord and may please him in every way: bearing fruit in every good work, growing in the knowledge of God, being strengthened with all power according to his glorious might so that you may have great endurance and patience, and joyfully giving thanks to the Father, who has qualified you to share in the inheritance of the saints in the kingdom of light.

(Colossians 1:9-12, NIV)

Concluding Remarks

Nestled in a valley high in the Alps is the town of Zermatt, Switzerland. Few places on earth can compare with Zermatt for beauty of natural surroundings. On a clear day tourists look above the village, and suddenly they espy the face of the Matterhorn pushing its sun-drenched rocky face into the deep blue heavens. The sight is breathtaking.

But on more days than Zermatt's Chamber of Commerce would like to admit, thick clouds roll through the high mountain passes, completely covering the Matterhorn's face from even the most intrepid tourist's binoculars. Not a few tourists have spent their precious vacation days in Zermatt without ever catching a glimpse of the Matterhorn.

In a similar fashion we might not be able to perceive the beauties of righteousness even though they are real. The pollution of sin can cut down our spiritual visibility and distort our vision. We think we perceive things as they are, but we do not. In a marvelous passage of the *Institutes* (I, 1, 2), the sixteenth-century Reformer John Calvin makes the point well:

> It is evident that man never attains to a true self-knowledge until he has previously contemplated the face of God, and come down after such contemplation to look into himself. For (such is our innate pride) we always seem to ourselves just, and upright, and wise, and holy, until we are convinced, by clear evidence, of our injustice, vileness, folly and impurity. Convinced, however, we are not, if we look to ourselves only, and not to the Lord also—He being the only standard by the application

of which this conviction can be produced. For, since we are all naturally prone to hypocrisy, any empty semblance of righteousness is quite enough to satisfy us instead of righteousness itself. And since nothing appears within us or around us that is not tainted with very great impurity, so long as we keep our mind within the confines of human pollution, anything which is in some small degree less defiled, delights us as if it were most pure: just as an eye, to which nothing but black had been previously presented, deems an object of a whitish, or even of a brownish hue, to be perfectly white.... But should we once begin to raise our thoughts to God, and reflect what kind of Being he is, and how absolute the perfection of that righteousness, and wisdom, and virtue, to which, as a standard, we are bound to be conformed, what formerly delighted us by its false show of righteousness, will become polluted with the greatest iniquity; what strangely imposed upon us under the name of wisdom will disgust by its extreme folly.

Our mind's eye has become polluted.

How do we begin to recover the spiritual sight taken from us by the Fall? We must experience a spiritual new birth (John 3) and repent of our sins. We recall that Luther began to understand the God who is really there once he had experienced the new birth (see chap. 7). He discovered that the all powerful, righteous God is one in the same with his loving heavenly Father.

We must also have our minds renewed constantly by the Holy Spirit. As the renewing of our mind proceeds, our spiritual vision begins to clear (see chap. 4). Although we remain sinner-saints and see through a glass darkly, we are able to understand more fully that the Bible's teachings about the living of life reflect God's own perspectives and standards of righteousness.

We must obey Christ's commandments. Our Lord declared: "If you love Me, you will keep My commandments" (John 14:15). We begin to apply the Scriptures as an infallible rule of faith and practice to everyday ethical decisions (see chap. 8). The old hymn is right: to be happy in Jesus, we must trust and obey.

The fellowship of like-minded believers becomes something we seek rather than something we dutifully endure or shun (see chap. 5).

We delight in our devotional life because it affords us with times of special communion with our wonderful Lord (see chaps. 2, 3, and 6). It is meaningful, not mindless.

The beauty of holiness comes into sharper focus. And a glimpse at God's own holiness makes us understand how blinded we were to our own sinfulness and rebelliousness.

Finally, we begin to understand why our Lord is so deserving of worship: not only is He very God, but He has done so much for us in sending His dear son Christ Jesus to die on the cross for our sins. How can we not but fall down on our knees in heartful thanks to our loving heavenly Father for our wonderful Savior? Hearts overflowing with thankfulness cannot help but worship.

The renewing of our minds, then, is pivotal for each one of us as we face the challenge of living faithfully in modern America. If our minds are being renewed constantly by the Holy Spirit, then we will retain our saltiness and light as we seek to minister to any of our neighbors who suffer from spiritual or material want. And if our minds are being renewed constantly by the Holy Spirit, we shall be able to love our brothers and sisters as ourselves and thereby indicate to a watching world that we are, indeed, Christ's disciples:

> A new commandment I give to you, that you love one another, even as I have loved you, that you also love one another. By this all men will know that you are My disciples, if you have love for one another.
>
> (John 13:34-35)

And perhaps if we are that kind of disciple, the paradox of which Chuck Colson spoke will begin to disappear.

Index of Subjects

Index of Persons

Index of Scriptures

Moody Press, a ministry of the Moody Bible Institute, is designed for education, evangelization, and edification. If we may assist you in knowing more about Christ and the Christian life, please write us without obligation: Moody Press, c/o MLM, Chicago, Illinois 60610.